Supporting
Children
through
Grief & Loss

Supporting Children through Grief & Loss

Practical Ideas and Creative Activities for Schools & Carers

Anna Jacobs

HINTON HOUSE Therapeutic Resource

HINTON HOUSE

First published in 2013 by

Hinton House Publishers Ltd, Newman House, 4 High Street,
Buckingham, MK18 1NT, UK
T +44 (0)1280 822557   **F** +44 (0) 560 3135274
E info@hintonpublishers.com

www.hintonpublishers.com

British Library Cataloguing in Publication Data
A CIP catalogue record for this book is available from the British Library.

ISBN 978 1 906531539

Printed and bound in the United Kingdom by Hobbs the Printers Ltd

FSC
www.fsc.org
MIX
Paper from
responsible sources
FSC® C020438

Contents

Activities

Enabling Feelings

Anger

Sadness

About the Author

Anna Jacobs is a qualified play therapist and creative arts therapist/counsellor, who is passionate about the needs of bereaved children and young people. She has been supporting bereaved children and their families for more than fifteen years, and has been a therapist and counsellor for more than twenty-five years. She has established and co-ordinated two pioneering Children & Young People's Services in the fields of cancer and palliative care in Lancashire & Cumbria and the South West of England.

Anna has supported children and families with many different types of loss, including serious illness, divorce and separation, sudden loss, extreme forms of bereavement such as murder and suicide, as well as those losses experienced within the care system. She has offered numerous trainings to social care, school and health staff and foster and adoptive carers on attachment theory, bereavement and loss. Her vision has always been that every child will have access to excellent local bereavement services and that every professional and family can understand the needs of children who have experienced loss.

She is the author of *Supporting Teenagers through Bereavement & Loss* as well as *Rory's Story*, *Lucy's Story* and *Changes*, therapeutic stories with exercises to help teenagers, children and the very young to understand the experience of loss and bereavement. She is the co-author, with Lorna Miles, of *Supporting Fostered & Adopted Children through Grief & Loss*.

Introduction

You would know the secret of death. But how shall you find it unless you seek it in the heart of life?

(Khalil Gibran, *The Prophet*, 1923)

One thing is certain in our lives: eventually we will die. Another thing that is equally certain is that, at some point, we will experience the death of a person close to us. The experience of losing a person to death is called loss – but loss can also come from other causes, such as separation, divorce and emigration.

Generally, in society, we regard children as having less to do with loss than adults. That is to say, we do not normally expect children to have a deeper experience of loss in their early lives. They may experience the death of a pet, they may experience a small separation and they may experience the loss of a grandparent, who may or may not be close to them. It is less common to experience the loss of a parent, parental figure or sibling.

However research published by Shipman et al. (2001) found that 79 per cent of all schools had children on roll who had been bereaved of a close family member within the previous two years. Harrison and Harrington (2001) estimated that, by the age of 16, six per cent of young people would have experienced the death of a parent. In addition, Silverman and Worden (1992) found that two years after a parental death self-esteem was significantly lower among bereaved children. These are not insubstantial figures and show that a significant number of children and young people do experience a more profound loss than society assumes – and are potentially deeply affected by it.

Within the history of childhood loss there is no clear model for supporting children in bereavement. In Victorian times, when death and loss were more commonplace, children took part in mourning rituals alongside their parents and relatives and the body of the deceased was normally viewed by all before being buried. More recently, children have not regularly been invited to funerals, even of their parents. Indeed, from approximately the beginning of the twentieth century parents began to regard children's attendance at funerals, and even acknowledgement of death, as inappropriate and irrelevant. Children just dealt with death and had to get on with it, without fully knowing what had happened. From this point onwards, particularly in the United Kingdom, we appear to have lost some of the language to explain death and the sense of loss resulting from it, as well as clear rituals that include children.

Those working with children and families are often confused about what to say, and how to support children who are bereaved or suffering a loss from another source. Yet with a few guidelines, clear suggestions and confidence most adults can be less fearful of what to say and what not to say. Children experience loss and grief in a very similar way to adults, yet we hesitate and stumble when we know a child has experienced loss. Do we say that someone has died? Do we ask how they are feeling? Do we ask if they went to the funeral? Do we check if they understand what death means? Do we check if they are seeing a parent if there has been a separation?

Children need opportunities to talk and play about what they see and experience and feel, because playing, talking and learning about their world is what children do in order to grow into healthy adults. Their experience of loss and grief, and the need to play, talk and understand this experience, is no different from other life experiences. However, there is a lack of confidence felt by some adults in broaching this subject. Sometimes this is due simply to lack of experience in using the language of loss. Death and dying in particular are still almost taboo subjects, and there is often a fear of upsetting those children who need to speak and share their loss and feelings with someone. At other times it is because the very act of speaking about the loss as an adult can remind that adult of the losses experienced during their own lives.

Loss itself is normal, however. When we love someone, we risk losing them. Adults know this and live with this. Children do not know this consciously and only learn it through beginning to experience loss. This happens very early, even as early as babyhood, when a mother walks out of the room and the baby cries deeply, feeling as if their world has ended. John Bowlby (1969) coined the term 'attachment' for the experience of babies bonding with their mothers, and added 'loss' to the title of his first treatise, as he perceived the two as inextricably linked in the experience of bonding between parent and child. When a child loses a parent, whether it is to another room when they are very young, or through separation or even death, this is loss in its basic primeval form, and all human beings are prepared for it from a young age. It is innate in us, as human beings, to experience loss, just as we experience life, love, death, the deeper feelings of fear and, hopefully, courage. However, children (whose experience of loss should be minimal when younger) can be supported to manage losses that come unexpectedly, too young, or with great damage to their lives, or simply if their temperament is unprepared for such losses. This book should help you to provide that support.

Through the work of organisations such as the Childhood Bereavement Network (see Resources) and other excellent services within the UK, together with a growing body of theory on childhood bereavement, children experiencing loss are now more able to access support.

This book aims to add to the growing list of supportive literature in a clear, concise and straightforward way, so that those adults who wish to support children in their experiences of loss can begin to gain the skills, language and confidence to do so. It is a book that was inspired by many professionals, including teachers, who asked questions such as, 'How do I speak to a bereaved child?', 'What do I say?', 'Can I mention the word death?'. These questions have frequently been asked at training sessions or when support is being given to individual children in their schools and health clinics. The professionals asking the questions appeared to feel a lack of confidence and showed the hesitancy that often exists when attempting to support children who are bereaved or have experienced a significant loss. Therefore it felt timely to offer a comprehensive guide to supporting children with bereavement and loss, which is easily accessible and useable.

Who is this book for?

This book is intended for those working with children between the ages of 5 and approximately 11 years who have experienced some form of loss. Although bereavement is the major loss referred to, there are of course other significant losses that a child may experience during the course of their life. The separation and divorce of parents, a parent going to prison or into the armed forces, and other losses (such as moving house or the loss of a pet) are all highly significant for children. Although it could be said that the impact of bereavement is greater than that of the other losses, this would clearly depend on the situation and circumstances, as for children all losses can be traumatic or life changing. Other losses can have the same impact as bereavement, since by their very nature they cause change and instability that threatens a child's fundamental sense of safety. It is possible, however, that with enough support from those around them, children can cope and continue to thrive.

Although the book has been written primarily to support teachers, teaching assistants and SENCOs (Special Educational Needs Coordinators) who are supporting a grieving child in a school environment, it can also be used by health professionals, social services professionals and parents or other carers.

How to use this book

The aim of the book is to guide adults through the different aspects of loss in which children will need support, and to give guidance on monitoring their own situation to decide if extra support might be appropriate. The first chapters give a background to theories of loss and bereavement, particularly Chapter 1: Theories of Bereavement & Loss and Chapter 2: How Death is Understood at Different Ages & Stages of Development. The following chapters offer more direct guidance: Chapter 3 looks at the questions children ask and how to answer them and Chapter 4 examines the different ways children express loss and how you can support them. Chapter 5 offers practical suggestions for helping children suffering a loss and Chapter 6 provides a toolkit of exercises and practical, creative activities.

Guidance is given for using the exercises, including how to approach them, when they are appropriate for groups, class or individual use, as well as ideas about how to introduce them into your own situation. The activities are photocopiable resources designed to cover different categories of need; they deal with feelings, memories, telling the story of the loss, and children's questions about loss. Exercises are a very valuable method of supporting children with the different aspects of loss, and by using them professionals, parents and guardians can become confident in supporting the needs of bereaved children or others experiencing different forms of loss. The book ends with a resources section (Chapter 7) that includes useful templates for schools, websites and descriptions of other books that may be of help.

At school

In school this book can be used both to inform support for children experiencing loss in the school environment and to offer some activities related to bereavement and loss; many of the activities are particularly well suited to the classroom. It can be used for guidance on how a school can respond to the bereavement or loss, as well as for staff training.

School professionals may want to use different parts of this book at different times, depending on the losses experienced and the needs and community in which the school is based. The exercises on specific feelings (Chapter 6: A Toolkit of Activities) can be used within circle-time sessions or at a difficult time within the classroom if a child is known to have experienced a significant loss. They can also be used, where indicated, to offer support to an individual child who has been bereaved or undergone a significant loss. For children who are offered individual support, various points will need to be remembered, for example: you should check with the child if they are comfortable with being seen as 'different' by being taken out of class *before* this happens; be discreet with support, particularly if the bereavement or loss is very recent; check who the child feels they could most easily turn to in the school and give the child special permission to seek out this person, if appropriate, during the day; ensure the room/venue where they are seen individually is a place where they feel safe, such as a SENCO's room, a library or a head's room; and check if the child wants the other children to know why they are going out of class, because some children like to have adults tell their classmates, while others prefer to tell their friends themselves.

Chapter 3: Questions Children Ask & How to Answer Them, can be very helpful when a teacher or other school professional wishes to know enough to respond in a classroom situation or in individual cases of particular loss. All children will be curious when one of their peers has lost a parent, or has experienced a separation, and naturally that curiosity spills over into questions. As many adults find these questions difficult to answer, this is one of the key chapters of this book for schools. Remember always to check what the child involved wishes others to know, and also what their family wants from the school. Being discreet and honest is usually the best way to support such families at times of stress. If a child asks these questions openly, it is always advisable to find a quiet place to talk, if possible, so that these difficult questions can be answered. Children who are stressed or grieving will invariably find it hard to absorb the answers and may well return to them at a later stage. Demonstrating to both children and their families that you can show sensitivity, even in a school environment, creates a sense of trust and safety that can lead to later support when needed.

Creating an assembly when someone in the community has had a particular loss can also be a beneficial way to support a child and family. See Chapter 5: How to Help and Chapter 7: Resources (Plan for a General Assembly on Bereavement) for more details on how to facilitate an assembly on bereavement and/or loss.

Care settings

Those professionals who are given the task of looking after children out of school hours and when parents work, including child minders and after-school clubs, will also find this book helpful when encountering children who have experienced loss. They may find Chapter 4: The Different Ways Children Express Loss & How to Support Them particularly helpful for signs of a child needing more support, as well as Chapter 3: Questions Children Ask & How to Answer Them. These professionals may also wish to look at Chapter 6: A Toolkit of Activities if they wish to incorporate any activities within their settings. Of course, as the child's carer rather than teacher, they may choose simply to give support by speaking with the child or understanding what their needs are, rather than actually offering activities related to their loss. They may also find support and help in the book when talking to the families who are experiencing loss.

Social care staff who offer support to children with more complex needs, such as those going into foster care, may wish to read the chapters on theory and understanding of death and loss at different ages (Chapters 1 & 2) to help inform them in their work with children whose loss has led to challenging experiences. Many children who are in contact with social care have experienced multiple losses and will therefore be experiencing many of the symptoms and aspects of loss discussed in this book. By supporting them with even one of their losses, social care staff could make some difference to the way in which these children begin to face their future. The individual exercises could be used appropriately by foster carers or social care staff in a range of situations. Alternatively, the theory and other background chapters in the first part of the book can support professionals and others in their understanding of how loss affects children, whether or not bereavement has occurred.

At home

Parents and carers, such as guardians, have a particularly difficult task when children are experiencing loss, sometimes because they themselves are also bereaved or grieving, or perhaps because they are, in some part, responsible for the loss; this may be the case in separation or divorce, or when a parent is going away on armed forces duty. Obviously, all parents do the best they can to support their children and no blame should be attached if parents choose to make the most difficult decisions, such as to separate or to leave home to follow a career. However, all parents can support their children fully while they cope with the impact of these decisions, and usually wish to do so.

Chapter 4: The Different Ways Children Express Loss & How to Support Them and Chapter 5: How to Help can be particularly useful in helping parents to identify if their children are in need of extra support. Chapter 3 looks at how to answer common questions that children ask, while Chapters 4 and 5 give indications of what to look out for and how to help, something parents regularly ask professionals. Many of the suggestions are both logical and unsurprising, although parents (as do professionals) often worry about how to talk about death and loss and how to support their children. It is helpful for all adults, including parents, to remember that children prefer honesty, to be kept informed even if the news is painful, and that they need ways to express their feelings safely in a supportive, loving atmosphere. Children will also benefit from preparation if changes occur as a result of losses, such as moving house.

Of course, it could be surprising for parents to hear that for children the experience of bereavement is similar to their experience of loss caused by separation and divorce. Loss, as mentioned above, is a normal and regular part of life, even if it sometimes happens earlier than most families would wish it to, and it is important to reassure them that, although loss may occur, most children do survive it fairly well with enough support and love. Indeed, many families these days are step-families, sometimes combining two or three different families, and the children do survive and thrive in most cases. The most important role for parents is to support their children with their love and care and to keep them safe, a job only parents, family members and guardians can do well. Sometimes this can be overlooked in the anxieties of what to say and how to say it, so it is worth being reminded of this when family life becomes stressful and tough. There are very few parents who cannot support their children with a little extra guidance. You can also look at the toolkit exercises in Chapter 6, as there may be some particular activities that appeal to parents, whether you are creative or not. Some of these exercises can be done together with the child or as a family.

This resource need not be read through from cover to cover. It is a manual that offers simple, clear ways to understand and support children, and will give adults greater confidence in doing so. By the end of the book most adults should feel confident enough to offer at least some support when a child they know is suffering from bereavement or loss.

Chapter 1
Theories of Bereavement & Loss

Research into the field of childhood bereavement and loss has been expanding since the 1980s, with a growing body of work focusing both on the theory behind loss and the way in which children can be best helped. This chapter describes some of these theories; it is not definitive or fully comprehensive, rather it is simply an introduction to some of the most influential ideas that have formed the baseline for this book. For those who are interested, more information can be found in the final chapter, References.

There are broadly three aspects of bereavement examined by theorists in research: firstly the process of grieving and its stages; secondly the determinants, or reasons, why there may be a varying experience of grief; and finally the factors that are found to be helpful in the grieving process.

Processes of grief

Within the first category writers such as Elizabeth Kübler-Ross and William J. Worden are significant. Kübler-Ross is well known for her seminal work, *On Death and Dying* (1969), which suggested that grieving moves through successive stages of denial, anger, bargaining, depression, and finally acceptance. Although no longer regarded as necessarily occurring in this sequence, those who have suffered loss or grief can certainly acknowledge that these are all phases they recognise from their own journeys into and beyond grief. The stages are self-explanatory, but of course are often not experienced as distinctly as described by Kübler-Ross.

William Worden, writing in his book *Children and Grief* (1996), expanded on Kübler-Ross's work and identified what he termed 'tasks for mourning'. These are:

1 accepting the reality of loss;
2 experiencing the pain of grief;
3 adjusting to an environment where the deceased is missing; and
4 re-investing emotional energy.

Elements of both these theories can be readily recognised in the process of loss with adults. Within children's loss, however, these stages or tasks may be less obvious, but it is just as necessary for them to be experienced in order for grief to be an appropriate means of surviving the mourning process. Theories such as these have influenced the services that now exist for children who have been bereaved. They are used as a guide for practitioners when monitoring the progress of grief, indicating the levels of support to offer and what to look out for. Such theories also help by acknowledging that children will, for example, become angry at one point, or show denial that the loss has happened, which is then reassuring for both carers and professionals as they offer ongoing support to bereaved children.

Determinants of grief

One of the main theories relevant to bereavement and loss today is that of attachment theory. Originating with John Bowlby (1969) this theory relates to the bond all human babies and children naturally make with their carers. The theory proposes that all children need to bond to at least one caring, empathetic, responsive adult in order to thrive. There are a number of styles of attachment, known as insecure or secure, and these have been found to correlate with the success or otherwise of a child to thrive, to manage their feelings and emotions, to have good self-esteem, and to grieve appropriately. It appears that the more secure a child is within the attachment relationship, the healthier is any grieving process for child. This is confirmed by Stokes (2004) who identifies one of the eight important points affecting the grieving process as, 'the nature of the attachment ... [divided into] ... the strength of the attachment ... the security of the attachment ... [and] the ambivalence of the relationship'. Stokes succinctly links theory and practice in her ground-breaking book, by examining how Winston's Wish (the well-known childhood bereavement charity that she founded) offers its support and the way in which this support is firmly based on some of the more influential theories such as attachment theory.

Attachment theory continues to be influential in the field of bereavement and loss with children; many theorists have developed Bowlby's ideas and examined how the attachment between carers and child affects the child as they grow into adulthood. It has been found, for example, that those children who have secure attachments to their parents and carers, that is to say who are successful, safe and secure in themselves and at an appropriate level developmentally, are more successful in their ability to grieve appropriately, manage their feelings and successfully move beyond this to healthy adulthood (Dyregrov, 1991). Although they may feel the feelings of grief and mourn deeply, they also recover and adjust more simply, as they have a more secure foundation on which to base this challenging experience. Resilience is a prime factor in bereavement, and it could be said that this basis of secure attachment offers a better chance for growing resilience in a child, as challenge is one of the factors that builds resilience (Stokes, 2004). Adults who were insecurely attached as children, perhaps with a loss that had never fully been resolved, can be less resilient when they experience further losses and challenges in their lives. This indicates that there is great value to be placed on supporting children when their losses first appear in order that they may become resilient adults.

When studying resilience and bereavement, five factors associated with resilience in children were compared by Schuurman to seven factors or characteristics of bereavement (2003). Schuurman noted that whereas bereaved children tend to have lower self-esteem, resilient children have high self-esteem. Similarly, resilient children tend to have a more easy-going temperament and be affectionate, whereas bereaved children can have higher levels of anxiety and fearfulness together with some evidence of depression. By promoting resilience in children, therefore, the needs of bereaved children, who have a predisposition not to be resilient, can be helped and monitored.

A newer and growing body of theory is that of neuroscience and how it relates to children who experience trauma and loss (Perry & Hambrick 2008). Research has shown that, during periods of stress, the parts of the brain that are affected by stress (the frontal lobes) become charged with chemicals that inhibit a child's ability to empathise or recognise their own emotions clearly. For a child who is experiencing deep loss, such as that of losing a parent, the frontal lobes may be temporarily charged with the chemical cortisone, which is known to cause aggression, mood swings and other behavioural aspects of loss exhibited at home and in the classroom. However, researchers have also shown that when children are offered empathy, care and support for their experiences, the frontal lobes calm down, the chemicals change to endorphins, which are 'feel-good' chemicals, and the child can then use this support to enable a management of what can seem to adults to be 'out-of-control' feelings and actions.

This particular research is very interesting, as it shows that the brain responds chemically to triggers in our environment, such as trauma and loss, and that emotion and empathy shown to a child will enable a change in these chemical responses. Research has examined children who have never experienced empathetic loving care (those who have experienced only different and repeated loss in their lives), and their brains have been found to be underdeveloped in the frontal lobes. Although research in neuroscience is evolving daily, this is a wonderful example of how it proves the value of support for children experiencing loss. The research also reveals that growing, childhood brains are more elastic and subject to change, unlike adult brains which are more fully formed, and this also supports the growth of services for bereavement that can enable such children to survive even quite traumatic loss with some success (Sunderland, 2008).

Helping the grieving process

The final aspect of the theory of bereavement, which relates to what has been found to be helpful to the bereaved, is found (for example) in the theory of continuing bonds (Klass et al., 1996). This theory states that children continue to reframe memories of the person who is deceased, along with feelings, which they then refer back to at key points in their lives in order to maintain the emotional bond that was there before the loss. This enables a healthy continuation of their growth and development. Continuing bonds theory guides practitioners in the use of memory boxes and books to enable the child to retain objects and memories associated with the person they have lost; by this means they maintain the important connection and can return to it as necessary. It also helps explain why children need to make Mother's Day cards, for example, even though their mother may be no longer alive.

Another theory influential in children's bereavement services is that of Stroebe and Schut (1999) who suggested there can be two aspects to the grieving process, which can be interrelated. The first is 'loss-orientation', which enables a child or adult to stay with the grief and focus on the pain in order to manage it. The second is 'restoration-orientation', in which a person is focused more on the ways of dealing with loss by being practical, thinking of the future and perhaps not enabling the feelings to emerge. Stroebe considered that the most healthy form of grief was one in which the two aspects co-occurred, and the person or child was able to 'oscillate' between the two. This theory can influence services that enable children to both plan for the future, which is much needed when they are grieving and they need to know what will happen next in their lives, and to face their pain. As children quite naturally do what could be called 'puddle jumping' (Stokes, 2004) within their grieving process, this is another theory that informs the support offered to children and can also be helpful in monitoring that success.

As can be seen from the outline above, these theories cover different aspects of bereavement and loss, and incorporate within them many ideas that are discussed in this book. Knowing that the information, ideas and exercises found here have a sound, theoretical basis will be helpful to those parents and professionals in schools and other services who wish to use the book for supporting bereaved children.

As a result of using this resource it is hoped that more children who are bereaved, or who have experienced loss in another form, will gain the support they need. New research continues to demonstrate the impact that bereavement can have on children if they do not receive such support. It is hoped, therefore, that this book can be regarded as a valuable addition to the library of emotional literacy for all professionals, parents and carers working to support children, so that bereavement and loss become better understood and adults can gain more confidence in supporting those children who experience loss.

Chapter 2

How Death is Understood at Different Ages & Stages of Development

To live in this world

you must be able
to do three things:
to love what is mortal;
to hold it

against your bones knowing
your own life depends on it;
And, when the time comes to let it go,
to let it go.

Mary Oliver, 'In Blackwater Woods', 1983

In general children understand death in a different way from adults, although they have exactly the same range of feelings. Therefore children at different ages will have different concepts and beliefs about what death means. As regards loss, children may, for instance, understand that a person has left, but will not understand that they will not return. Developmentally, until the age of 5 to 7, children have little concept of permanence and therefore will not understand (particularly when a loss is due to death) that the person concerned is not coming back.

Death can be complicated for adults to understand, therefore it can be helpful to consider how children's perception may be dependent on their own developmental stage. Younger children in particular will find it hard to understand the concept of death, whereas older children may have a clearer knowledge that death happens and is forever, and so may need different levels of information regarding what death actually is. Suggestions for such information are given in more detail below, but can include telling a child that a person's body no longer works, that the person cannot see, hear, breath, walk, and so on, and that they will never again be able to do this as their body has stopped working. For older children spiritual understandings and beliefs about what happens at death are also part of the meaning-making when a death occurs in their lives.

When the loss is connected to a separation, divorce, or other cause, children may understand that someone is not coming back to live with them, but may struggle to understand why. A child of three may return to the question of 'Where is daddy or mummy?' for a long period of time until they realise the person is not coming back, whereas older children will need both reassurance that the separation is not due to anything they have done, and perhaps also an outline of what has led to the divorce, move of employment or other reason for loss. It is important to explain in simple language what has caused the person to go away: for example, what led to the divorce or why a job has taken a family member away.

When a child of a very young age hears that an adult (especially someone who they care for and trust) is not coming back, they will normally think this is due to something that they have done since their world is egocentric; that is to say, they perceive their world as if they are at its centre. For this reason, when a young child is told of a loss they also need to know that it is not their fault, and that nothing they have done has caused the loss.

Parents, carers and educational or other professionals can help to support children to understand the meaning of death generally, and their reactions both to death and other losses, by helping them to understand at the level they are ready for. Bereavement and loss can be openly discussed within general lessons and through using books such as this one, and appropriate support can be arranged when needed.

This chapter is divided into different ages and stages, beginning with some developmental milestones for each stage. As these stages are not clear-cut, there is some overlap in the chronological ages. This is followed by discussion of how children understand death and loss, and the implications of their understanding. Some suggestions of what to say are also given. Although suggestions for discussion are given in each section, their use will depend on the level and sophistication of understanding in individual children, as each child develops at different rates. It is therefore worth checking the different sections when looking for examples of what to use.

Age 1 to 5: Little understanding of death and its permanence

Babies and toddlers are emerging into a world that is very new to them. They depend completely on the adults around them, and in order to thrive they need to bond to at least one empathetic, loving adult. They respond quite physically to many stimuli, and are learning continually what the world is made of and their place in it. They are learning to walk, talk and play, as well as the basics of potty training, how to understand others and their place in their family. Families are the centre of their lives for at least the first year or two, and babies who attend nurseries and child-minding facilities (as well as those with nannies and au pairs) will see these extra people as extended family members. Although there is usually little clear verbal contact before approximately 18 months to 2 years, babies as young as a few days old have been shown to understand what is happening around them, though it may not be at the level of understanding that an older child or adult has. Babies are shown to respond to known adults with smiles and gazes almost from birth and clearly recognise their carers almost from the day that they are born. From birth to over 18 months in particular the process of attachment or bonding is taking place with one or more significant carers, and this is the most important process in enabling a child to grow up healthy and happy.

From the age of 2 to 3 years, children are learning to adapt to the world around them beyond the family. They are learning to talk, walk, socialise and regulate their feelings and begin to establish their characters. They are preparing to attend school and to adapt to that environment, and are usually keen to learn. They are moving through the stage of having tantrums and exploring their ability to shape their world. They are also learning the limitations of their power, both the power of their emotions to change things and their power of behaviour and manipulation, hence the testing times of tantrums. Beyond the age of 3 to 4 most of this stage is normally achieved successfully. However, if a significant loss occurs during this time, it can disrupt this stage of development and leave a child 'stuck' in the phase of attempting to regulate their emotions and their belief in their ability to shape the world around them.

Implications

Although this stage covers quite a large range of age and development, the needs of these children are generally the same. Younger children tend to need reassurance that life will continue as normal, therefore routine discipline, life patterns and activities need to be emphasised in order for a child to be reassured that 'life goes on'. In addition, any reinforcement of the child's feelings of safety and security are vital at this stage of development.

When very young children under 5 years old experience loss and death, they may return to needing explanations again and again, something many parents and professionals can find confusing. At this age they tend to ask questions such as, 'Where have they gone?' and 'What does death mean?' These questions are so very hard for adults to answer, but trying to be honest about the fact that adults do not have all the answers, while explaining that different people have different ideas of where people go at death (such as heaven and into the stars) can help a child to adjust. Answers to these questions could include: 'Your daddy has died, which means he cannot come back, but you can keep asking me as I know how hard it is to believe that'; or 'When someone dies this means their body stops working, they cannot walk, talk, see, move, breathe or do any of the things our bodies do.'

Death and loss can also be explained by referring to the cycles of life and death in nature. For example: 'You know that in nature the leaves turn brown in winter and die, well just like that animals and people die eventually, and sometimes they die sooner than we want them to. This is what has happened to [deceased's name].' If a family believes in a particular faith or are willing for the concept of heaven to be introduced, a child can be told where a bereaved relative has gone by mentioning their particular faith, or by saying something like: 'Some people believe that when a person dies, they go to a place called heaven; what do you think heaven looks like?'

When a separation or divorce occurs, the child will probably want to know what will happen to them and who they will live with, as well as the reason for the divorce. It is usually best to say something very simple at this stage such as: 'Mummy and Daddy have decided we cannot live together any more. Sometimes that happens even with people who love each other, but you know we will always love you and do what is best for you.' Loss of a parent due to a career move could be explained in the following way: 'Do you remember we told you that Daddy might have to go away for a while for his work? Well, he is going to be away for quite a long time as he is going to a country called [name of country] and will not be able to come home for a while. We can keep in touch with him by email and phone calls, however.'

Whatever the cause of their loss, children need to know where they will be living and some of the practicalities of what will happen to them, since any loss brings a degree of insecurity. Being reassured that they will remain where they live, or will see Daddy weekly, or will write letters and phone regularly, as well as knowing which school they will go to if they are moving, helps a child to understand as well as adjust to the losses.

It is also very important to keep checking if children would like to ask their own questions when they are being told about their loss and to reassure them that they can ask and check things at any time they want. They will also need to be reminded that anything that has happened is not their fault.

Age 5 to 7 (or later): Greater understanding of death and the beginning of an understanding that death is permanent

At this age children are starting to have a sense of themselves and the world around them. The child's attachment to their family is still very significant, as it helps determine their sense of security in their family, their empathy towards others, their ability to learn and grow happily, and their ability to use all of their new experiences to learn about themselves and the world. Their self-esteem is also determined by these things. Peer relationships will be growing in importance, as will their experience of school. The child is continually learning about the world and their place in it as they move slowly beyond the confines of their family. They will also be gaining confidence verbally and physically, unless there are specific disabilities. Emotions are very deeply felt at this age, and tantrums can come and go as a younger child works out what they can and cannot control.

Children at this age, particularly the later years of this stage, will be using play to make sense of the world, both in dramatic play (e.g., role-playing scenarios of house and family, teacher and learning, and the use of fantasy figures such as princes and princesses, fairy stories and make-believe) and other play, such as having fun in sand and paint. They have what is known as 'magical thinking', meaning the child believes that things they do or say can transform life, and are trying to distinguish between reality and fantasy; this is the beginning of the special time for fairy stories and myths. Children are still not fully able to use cognitive or conceptual thinking and language: that is to say, thinking and language that contains concepts not directly related to their lives or their concrete experiences, but which is rather symbolical or more intellectual.

Death is becoming more understood as permanent at this stage, though there will be various levels to this understanding. Children over 5 years old may grasp that death happens, although they may not have ever experienced it. Some children will have experienced the loss of a pet, and some may have already experienced loss, such as a separation or death of a grandparent. They may still need to check their understanding on a regular basis and may need explanations similar to those given above for younger children with regard to what may happen at death and what people believe. However, they may also connect these explanations with their experience, even if it is an experience of something as simple as a fly dying, or a leaf turning brown.

With regard to other losses, children will be more aware of the separation that may occur through divorce, as by this stage they are attending nursery or school and some of the other children will be living in single-parent households or with step-families. Children will become more alert to others' experience and so this will be something they can compare with their own experience. However, they will still question if a separation is actually their fault or whether or not it is permanent. Children at this age will also need clear and simple explanations. Other losses such as a parent leaving for military service, or to go to prison, are difficult experiences for such young children, who again will struggle to understand that the loss is not their fault, though with clear explanations this can be avoided.

Implications

At this age most children will have a reasonably secure relationship to at least one carer. Any loss, especially if it is the loss of this carer, will particularly affect their level of security. They will probably continue to question what death is and find it hard to understand the permanence of their loss, though older children may be able to understand this more fully. They are likely to regress and to exhibit what is termed a type of 'bargaining' behaviour based on the magical thinking process in the hope that the loved one returns. Examples of such bargaining behaviour include being extremely good or finding ways of calling attention to themselves, in the hope that their behaviour brings their loved one back. Other examples can be behaving extremely badly, or becoming ill. All of these behaviours are unconscious ways in which a child may respond as a way of making sense of their loss or bereavement.

Children at this stage of development often blame themselves, believing they are the cause of the death or the separation. By using their magical thinking, children both believe that they are responsible for the loss and that perhaps they can do something to change the situation. For a time they will depend more completely on the person who is caring for them, as their reaction is often to revert to baby-like behaviour, even at the age of 6.

Examples of what to say at this stage can include some of the suggestions from the previous section. In addition it is always helpful to be honest if possible, for example: 'Your dad and I are separating. We have decided that though we love each other, we can no longer live together. We are very sorry about this and want you to know we will always love you and you will be able to choose how to keep in touch with both of us, who to live with and anything else'; and 'I am so sorry to have to tell you that your mother died this morning from an accident. This is the most terrible news for us all, and we want you to know that [I/your dad] will be looking after you, with the help of [your grandparents]. I can tell you more details if you want to know, but you will also be able to speak to someone separately if you need to.'

It is usually best to be clear about the cause of the loss, although if the loss is caused by death from suicide it can often be very hard to find the right words, because this is perhaps the most complicated form of loss for most children to understand. If there was no clear lead up to the loss, the best way to explain this is to say, for example: 'Your [father/mother] has died this evening. He/she chose to take his/her own life, as sometimes people find it too hard to stay alive and they become ill in their heads, making them choose things that are difficult for us as family to bear. He/she still loved you very much and did not want to hurt you, but he/she must have been in such terrible pain to choose to do this thing. We can tell you as many details as you need to know later, but not now. We can offer you someone to talk to and ask questions whenever you are ready.'

Suicide would be regarded as the most difficult type of loss to explain to any child and therefore it would normally be recommended that expert help and support would be sought in these instances.

Age 7 to 11: Full understanding of death as permanent, giving rise to questions about it

Children over the age of 7 years tend to have a more permanent sense of both themselves and life. Consequently they have a clearer understanding of the permanence of death. They are continuing to establish a personality, confidence and self-esteem, learning to read and write fully, and to establish friendships and life beyond the home. Although family is still the priority at this age, it changes over time as they become involved in other activities and socialise more with their peers. Children will hopefully have a more settled emotional life, with fewer tantrums and mood swings.

School will be a significant part of life for most children, with growth in learning, physical activities such as sports, and extra-curricular activities such as Cubs or Brownies, hobbies, and so on. Having a secure bond with one or more carers will then enable them to go out into the world more and explore their place in it. If they do not have a secure bond with their carers or are in the care system, for example, this can affect their experience of confidence and security to explore, experience other things and develop friendships and relationships. Those in the care system in particular will have known loss from an early age, due to the loss of their birth family, either temporarily via foster care or permanently via adoption. Children at this age are therefore growing physically, emotionally, socially, psychologically and cognitively.

At this age death is understood as being more or less permanent. A child from the age of 7, although they may still have some tendencies towards magical thinking, will usually grasp that death has happened and will need to know more. They will understand death more on the physical level (that the body is no longer breathing, cannot talk, walk or think), but they will also often have more profound questions about what it means – questions that do not occur to younger children. They like to be involved in all or some aspects of the process, such as the funeral or saying goodbye to the body of the person. In fact, children can often be less fearful of this than adults though they may still take time to fully accept their loss.

Children will understand more and more clearly at this stage the sources of the loss, whether from death or from other causes such as divorce or separation, prison, military service or even foster care. As children are becoming more aware of the world around them, some will be acutely aware of the existence of these sorts of losses, although the explanations for them are still important.

Implications

At this stage of development children will need to know more details, to have questions answered and to be dealt with honestly. They may be in deep shock or they may be more simply sad and angry. Their understanding will be of a more sophisticated variety, with some insights into how the adult world around them is affected. They may therefore show a lot more empathy to those around them, for instance towards their remaining parent if it is a parental death, and want to be more helpful. They are beginning to be less selfish generally in their responses, as the focus of their life is not quite so much on themselves as at the earlier stages. However, they will still need their own reassurances and have their own responses and regressions as in the other stages of development. Children will also need to know how their lives will change, who will be looking after them, and to have a sense of order and normality in their daily lives, which can be reassuring when death is affecting them.

Children aged between 7 and 11 will be more aware that loss, particularly from death, can cause them to feel different. This is particularly difficult for children of this age and stage, as they are developing closer relationships with their peers. The sense of isolation when a young person is aware that their mother or father can no longer attend parents' day, or activities such as a school play, will be felt profoundly. Whether the loss is from separation or divorce, prison or other, children who feel different always have a need to meet with others in a similar situation. Children at this age need to identify with other children and make strong friendships, sometimes lasting for life, therefore anything that inhibits that sense of growing friendship and connection can affect their sense of self-worth. However, in our society divorce and separation are more frequent, enabling most children to reduce that sense of isolation when a family does break down. There are, of course, other ways for children to feel a reduced sense of isolation due to their loss, in particular by reading books that discuss such losses, watching television programmes, reading and writing on websites or attending groups with others in a similar situation. It is also possible, as children reach this age and stage, that schools can play their part by using the exercises and other suggestions within this book to enable children to support each other whatever the cause of the loss.

Age 11 and over: Fuller understanding of death, including the need for questions and more involvement in the practicalities of the loss

Children over the age of 11, or those who have begun adolescence early, are more alert to the world, their place in it and their own identity and character. They have begun to enter the world of adolescence, with its focus on changing bodies, hormones, relationships and the future. They will have been exposed to more loss and change, either through television or family or their peer group, than at the earlier stages of development and are aware of what death and loss means, though they may not understand fully how it affects them. Their family is still significant at this age, and though it becomes less and less significant in everyday terms it is still the foundation for their future and vital to their emotional health and wellbeing. However, peers are becoming more and more important and influential, as well as more supportive.

Implications

Children of this age, though they understand the permanence of death, may not have experienced it first-hand. Therefore they may be shocked by their own emotional reactions and may need to regress, often to younger behaviour and a desire to take less responsibility in their lives. However, they also have a greater need to be involved in the process of mourning, for instance with the funeral arrangements. The tendency with this stage is to react in one of two ways: either to become more empathetic and act older than their years, becoming very responsible and sensible because they feel isolated or different, or to react with disbelief, rebel, begin to withdraw from life as it was before the loss, and possibly to take up a risk-taking behaviour, turning more to their peers than to their family. Both of these reactions are normal at first, and most children and young people will eventually revert. Children of this age with faith in a religion may lose that faith from a sense of anger at what has happened. Alternatively it can strengthen their faith. Children without faith, the majority of the population, may begin to question the more spiritual aspects of life and try to understand what death is. Their urge is normally to understand at a more profound level what has happened to their relative, alongside the urge to try and bring them back, as with younger children.

Other losses such as divorce and separation are also very difficult to understand for this age range, as children are just beginning to move beyond the boundaries of the home to explore their own peer groups and their sense of themselves in the world. When a loss such as divorce occurs, the foundation upon which their future is based is shaken and this can lead to some of the behaviours mentioned above. However, these children can more readily understand the needs for divorce and separation and can use clear explanations and honest feelings to make sense of this particular type of loss.

It can also be a more challenging time for the families of such children, since they will want to allow their young people to remain in contact with their relatives, even if they have moved away, gone to prison or left for other reasons. Children of this age will have their own clear opinions and preferences about what happens to them when their families separate and divorce, and it is important that these are heard and taken into account. If a family has a father or mother who has been put in prison, it is much harder to keep this from older children, although this is possible when children are younger. Some prisons now offer a service allowing letters to pass freely between children and their parents, enabling the attachment between them to be continued, even at a distance.

Conclusions

Having examined all of the developmental stages of children's understanding and some of the implications of these, it is important in conclusion to recognise that some points are important for children of any age:

1   Honesty is most important when explaining death and loss to all children.
2   Involvement is also important, whatever the cause of the loss.
3   Death and divorce will need explaining at different levels for different ages, but all children will need some explanation.

All children will have some reactions to loss, but most children can manage these losses with the support and guidance of adults who are informed by knowledge of the characteristics and needs of each stage of child development.

Chapter 3
Questions Children Ask & How to Answer Them

'What I said was, "Is anybody at home?"' called out Pooh very loudly. 'No!' said a voice and then added, 'You needn't shout so loud. I heard you quite well the first time.' 'Bother!' said Pooh. 'Isn't there anybody there at all?' 'Nobody.'

A.A. Milne, *Winnie-the-Pooh*, 1926

Children by their very nature are curious. Therefore when loss occurs from any cause, they will always have questions. They may not be obvious in their questions and may need to choose their moments carefully, as well as what to ask and how to ask it. But it can be accepted that all children will need to ask some questions, and it is usually helpful for adults to be prepared for these and to be able to provide answers.

As regards death some adults will be more confident than others in responding clearly, so try and be prepared in advance, reminding yourself that if you, as an adult, are open and honest about death and dying, then the children can respond more appropriately and adjust better to their loss.

Sometimes children experiencing the loss of their pet will have the same questions as a child who has lost a family member, because to them pets are family members. Obviously, in the case of a pet, discussions about what will happen to the child as a result of the loss are not appropriate, but the questions and ideas about death are the same and can be answered in a similar way. In fact, children who are able to face the loss of a pet are often better able to face more important losses when they are older.

Guidelines for professionals preparing to answer a child's questions

🖐 Allow the child to choose both the time and place for questions and ensure the child feels safe enough to ask their questions by offering a relaxing environment. If in school, ensure any questions or discussions do not take place in front of other children who may not understand either the question or the answer. This can be a room they are familiar with, such as a corner of a classroom or the head's room (if they have not had bad experiences of this).

🖐 Prepare the environment in advance. Your preparation can include having a friend nearby to support them or bringing a toy into school, for example, to help their sense of safety and security.

🖐 Always ask the child if they have any questions they would like to ask, after preparing as above. If in school, for example, suggesting that the child may have some questions about what has happened can be a great relief to a child who has not been able to ask anything previously. However, bear in mind that they may not wish to ask anything. Reassure them that they do not have to talk now if they do not want to, but make sure they know they can at any time if they wish.

🖐 Remember to assure the child they will not get into trouble for asking questions about their loss.

🖐 Never promise that you can answer all of the questions, but say you will try and answer as honestly as you can. If you do not know an answer, you can say so. You can also promise to try and speak to the child's parents or carers if the questions refer to issues only they will know.

Cooperating with a child's parents or carers

🖐 Occasionally you may find that a child uses their time with you to ask questions that are really more appropriate for parents or carers to answer. If this is the case, check if the child would like you to talk to their parents or carers. They may not want you to do this, as they may be concerned about the reaction. Sometimes they would like another person to talk to their parents or carers and have just been waiting for an opportunity to ask someone.

🖐 When contacting parents or carers, always try to hold a potentially difficult conversation face-to-face rather than on the telephone. Parents and carers will also be having a difficult time and may need preparation through an initial telephone call. Tell them their child has been asking questions, but then remember to offer sympathy for their loss – whatever the cause of this may be – before discussing these questions. Check with parents if the child has been asking any questions in the home. If necessary you could offer them the information for parents in this chapter to support them.

🖐 Reassure parents and carers that questions are normal when a child experiences loss and that you are working together with them to support their child.

🖐 Ask parents and carers if they would like to be the ones to answer any difficult questions. Ask them if there are any aspects of the loss they would prefer their child not to know yet. For example, when a loss is due to suicide it is often difficult to decide when is the right time to tell a child the cause of such a loss.

- Offer to keep in touch with a parent either by telephone or through meetings, in case there are more developments that professionals looking after children need to know about.

- If you do not find it possible to make contact with parents and carers, even after trying telephone calls or letters, do reassure the child that you will do all you can to try and answer their questions in the future.

Guidelines for parents and carers preparing to answer a child's questions

- Offer a quieter evening or use bedtime to have a talk with children. Make sure the child feels safe enough to ask any difficult questions. Safety usually involves a familiar environment, with people the child is familiar with and assurances that they will not get into trouble. It may be in a room at home that they are particularly comfortable in or with a particularly loved toy to hold.

- Alternatively, discussions and questions could be a family sharing time, particularly if there is more than one child in the family. Again ensure the children feel they can all ask questions, that they feel safe enough to ask difficult questions, and that they know they will not get into trouble by asking them.

- Always ask if a child has any questions, and encourage them to ask questions if they are unsure about anything. Some children will never ask questions unless prompted. Others will continually ask questions.

- Never promise you will have all the answers, but say you will certainly try to answer honestly anything that is asked.

- Offer the child more than one opportunity to ask questions, as children like to return both to questions and answers. Sometimes they need to ask the same question a few times. This usually serves to help them believe the answer if the question was on a difficult subject.

Cooperating with professionals and schools

- School professionals and others can be very helpful in preparing your child for the changes that occur as a result of loss. Questions are often asked at school to which a teacher or other member of staff may not know the answers. Therefore it is usually useful to keep in touch with school and to keep them up to date with what is happening at home.

- If your child has been asking difficult questions, try and warn their teacher that they have been doing so. If you can, tell them what these questions are, or you could write them down if you find it hard to talk about these things.

- Tell the school clearly how you would like them to answer certain questions relating to your child's loss. There are some questions that children ask which have a number of possible answers. Make sure you tell the school if there are some questions you do not want them to answer, perhaps related to a complicated loss or accident. Teachers can then refer your child back to you, as the parent, to answer these questions.

✋ Check with the school that they know facts that are relevant to your loss, so that questions asked at school can be answered appropriately. It is always your choice, as a parent or carer, to decide what you want to tell a school or other professional; however, by informing them of some of the details, teachers and other professionals can support your child more effectively when questions and concerns arise.

Common questions and suggested answers

Remember to keep your answers to any question both simple and appropriately honest. Both professionals and carers need to be mindful that children in distress at times of loss, just like adults, have less ability to concentrate. Always allow the child to repeat the question or to rephrase it; repeating a question usually indicates either that they have not understood your answer or that the answer is a difficult one to believe or accept.

The following questions and suggested answers cover some of the queries that a child can raise when death and loss have entered their lives. First, questions relating to a loss from death are examined, and then questions about other losses.

Questions about death

The most important point to remember when dealing with questions about death is to use honesty appropriately – it is better to speak of 'death' and 'dying' than to use euphemisms such as 'gone away' or even 'passed away'. Children can misinterpret these terms and be misled or, even worse, confused. Prepare yourself as these questions are ones that can raise huge emotional reactions in some people. Ask yourself if you are able to talk about death and dying to a child, and if not, why not? Talk to your colleagues for support if needed.

Question: 'What is death, Miss?'

Answers: Being asked to define death is the biggest question for most adults and it is very hard to answer, as we do not fully know ourselves, other than that death is the end of life. Children asking this question are asking a very fundamental question about life and our mortality in order to make sense of the absence of someone. Therefore they usually need to be reassured that the person is out of pain, will not return and has gone from this world. The first thing to say is:

> *'We don't fully know, as different people have different ideas of what it is, however, …'*

This can be followed in various ways, depending on the age of child and their concept of death:

> *'... death is when a body stops working, the person stops breathing, the person will no longer be able to talk, walk, breathe, move, or be alive in any way.'*

It is also possible to describe death with a reference to nature, such as:

> *'... death is the end of a life, just like when a leaf turns from green to brown.'*

Using examples from nature is often a good way of explaining what death is to children who do not fully understand its permanence. They may well ask this question several times, each time learning and understanding a little more about what death really means. If the person was ill, or was in an accident and took time to die, the child can be reassured that:

> *'... death means a person can no longer feel pain.'*

Question: 'Where has my daddy/mummy/gran/granddad gone?'

Answers: Children asking this question are also asking if their loved one is coming back. It is a part of the grieving process to try and understand where the person who has died has gone, and children can be greatly helped with clear answers related to their family's belief system. These days, many families are not a member of a faith community, so the answer will depend on who is being asked the question as well as the belief systems of the child's family. Those who come from traditions such as Christianity or Islam will be able to answer appropriately for the child:

> *'... to heaven, to another life, to nirvana, into a star.'*

For those who do not have a faith tradition, or if the family have not spoken to you about what they have told the child, it is often best to say something like:

> *'Well, people do not really know what happens when someone dies, but we know they are out of pain, and that the part of them that was in their body is no longer here.'*

Alternatively you could say:

> *'Sometimes people think that a person has a spirit or soul that continues to live somewhere, like heaven or in a star, but we also know that we can think of them as being partly still here in your heart.'*

It is also useful to say that:

> *'Nobody really knows what it looks like when someone dies or what heaven looks like; what do you think it looks like/where do you think they have gone?'*

It is then possible to allow children to show you in a drawing; make sure you have pens and paper to hand in case they are interested in doing so. When asking this question, children need to be reassured that the loss is not due to something they have done. For example:

> *'[Name of person] has gone away, not because they wanted to, or because of anything you did, but because they had to/because they were ill/had an accident.'*

Having some sense of where their loved person has gone, and a clear understanding that they cannot return, can greatly help in the bereavement process.

Question: 'Why did God take them away?' and 'Why have they died?'

Answers: Again this is a very difficult question as it forces us as adults to consider why people do die; why at *this* time, when a child is still young and needing their loved one? It is therefore very important when answering this question that you make sure the child knows that they are not to blame for their relative dying and that in most cases the relative did not wish to die. The answers to this question depend on both the cause of death and the faith of the family. For example:

> *'Your loved one died because they were ill/had an accident [cause of death]. But they did not want to go; their body simply could not work anymore.'*

If the cause of death is from suicide, a different answer is needed:

> *'Although it seems that your loved one chose to die at this time, we do know that they only did that as they were very ill in their head and thought it was the best way to be out of pain. They did not want to leave you, and had been ill for some time.'*

Alternatively you could say:

> *'We don't know why God took [name of person] away, nor why they died now when you really need them close by – but everyone has to die eventually, sometimes when they are young, sometimes when older, and this was the time for [name of person] to die.'*

In addition, if the family is a faith family, you could add:

> *'Your loved one was ready to go; we don't really know why, but God will now look after them in [heaven, or word from another faith] for you.'*

It is important when answering their questions to reflect how hard it is for children when someone very close to them has died, by saying such things as:

> *'It feels really hard to understand that someone has died.'*

Alternatively you could say:

'I guess you must feel very upset about all these questions you are asking.'

By reflecting some of the difficulties the child might be experiencing, you will encourage them to continue asking questions and to recognise some of the things they are feeling at a difficult time.

Question: 'What does heaven look like?'

Answers: Again this is a typical question from children who may or may not be from faith families. 'Heaven' is the concept that children are most often told about. Therefore it is often good to ask children what *they* think heaven looks like. It is amazing how many of them think it is populated by angels. We can then answer this question by saying, for example:

'Although no one really knows what heaven is like, we know it is a place where [name of person] will be at peace, out of pain, and well looked after.'

Angels are clearly a concept that children are happy with, and referring to angels if the child mentions them first is fine. What the children are really asking here is whether their relative is being looked after and safe; they are trying to visualise where the person is and to understand the indescribable; that is, where people go at death. Therefore, giving children a chance to say first how *they* visualise heaven and to concretise that image is often a way to support this question.

Question: 'What does it feel like when you die?'

Answers: Children ask this question to try and find out more about how their loved one feels about no longer being with them, but it is also a sign that their natural curiosity is prompting them to find out more about something new to them. They may or may not have viewed the body, and some children will have had a chance to touch their loved one and found the body to be cold at death. This happens more frequently when their relative has been ill and perhaps has been looked after in a hospice or another place.

Answering this question is difficult for adults, who must be honest about not knowing, while also trying to be sensitive to the reasons behind the questions. One of the most important answers can be:

'We don't know for sure what it feels like, as people cannot come back to tell us.'

And if you are confident enough to continue, you could add:

> *'Sometimes people who have nearly died but then remain alive say it is a lovely feeling, and that they knew they were safe and going to be with previous relatives who have died.'*

Alternatively you could say:

> *'Although nobody really knows what it feels like to die, we know that [person's name] is no longer in pain, and sometimes people have a very peaceful look on their faces just after death. We hope this means that wherever they go is a good place for them to be.'*

Sometimes children have seen the struggle to remain alive, for instance after an accident or at the end of a long illness. It is important, therefore, to follow any answers with a reminder that usually people do not want to die no matter how lovely it may feel, but that it was their time to do so. It is particularly important *never* to say that being dead is like a long sleep, as this can give children nightmares and stop them from having peaceful sleep themselves. It is always fine to admit that we adults do not know everything, and that there are some questions we cannot answer fully.

Question: 'Will he/she come back?' and 'Is death really forever?'

Answers: With this question children are asking the ultimate question: that is, how can they believe you when told their loved ones are not coming back and that death really is permanent? This question is particularly important since children watching television programmes or playing computer games will have come across stories of people returning from the dead. Younger children will still be learning that death is permanent and the differences between fantasies such as those seen on the television, and reality. The best answer therefore is:

> *'No, your relative cannot come back, as once someone has died they are no longer able to return to life.'*

However, this has to be qualified depending on both the age of the child and the nature of the loss. Follow this statement with one that reflects how a child may feel and empathise with their need to know for sure that the deceased person is not returning:

> *'I am sorry, but once someone is dead they can never come back and be alive again. It is hard to understand this, but over time I am sure you will come to believe it.'*

Your answer should also take into account that in some faith communities, such as Buddhism, there is a belief in reincarnation: that a person returns to life in another person or form. See Chapter 7: Resources for examples of books which helps explain other faith beliefs or cultural norms to children. If the child's family believes in reincarnation you can add:

'We hope [name of person] will come back in another body or form at some time in the future, but it will be very hard for us to know where and when that happens so we still have to accept that [name of person] has gone from us.'

Question: 'What did I do wrong that [name of person] had to die?' and 'Is it my fault, because we had an argument just before [name of person] died?'

Answers: Clearly this question relates to a child's belief in their part in the death or loss. Younger children, being at an egotistical stage of development, can believe that they can cause death. This belief can be compounded when something difficult has happened between them and their loved one before death. Therefore reassurance is vital to help the child understand that nothing they did made a difference and that they did not cause the death. An answer to this question could be:

'You did not do anything wrong to cause them to die. A child cannot cause people to die, it was [the illness, accident] that caused their death, and you must not blame yourself at all. It is not your fault.'

This may need to be repeated a number of times before a child believes it, in order that they can relax in the knowledge that the death was from another cause.

If the child had a difficult relationship with the person who died (very tempestuous, for example), or if the relationship was with a father or mother who did not always live with them, this feeling of responsibility may be bigger. For this reason you could add something like:

'No child has ever caused the death of an adult. However, I do understand that you did not always get on with [name of person], which may make you think you caused this to happen. No matter how difficult things were between you, remember that they loved you and did not want to leave you, and that nothing you did would have made a difference.'

This comment both reflects the complicated relationship that existed and emphasises the fact a child can never be the cause of death. It also offers the empathy to help a child begin to adjust to a loss that is bound to be complicated, because the relationship itself was complicated. This can sometimes be helped with extra support to ensure that any feelings of guilt are reduced.

Question: 'Why was he/she cold when I touched him/her?'

Answers: This is a very simple question with a very complicated answer! A child asking this will have said goodbye to their loved one, either before or after the death, but does not know the impact death has on a person's body. They are asking a fundamental question about life, as well as perhaps referring to feelings associated with losing the person. Therefore it is important both to answer this question simply and to reflect on the feeling behind it. For example:

> *'[Name of person] was cold because their body was no longer working. When a body is no longer working the blood does not go around and the breath stops. Because these things keep a living body warm, when they stop it makes the body cold. However, I guess it must have been hard for you to touch your loved one and find they felt so different. I hope it was not too scary and difficult for you.'*

Using this sort of answer allows the child to begin to understand the process of death, and also provides an opportunity to reflect on how the viewing of the body felt. Many children are happy to be near their loved ones at death if they are prepared in the right way by being told what to expect: that the body will not move, it will be cold, stiff, and so on. This gives the child a clear opportunity to say goodbye as well as to begin the process of accepting the death. This is true for both adults and children, but for children the need to say goodbye is particularly key when the person dying is a parent, carer, sibling or very close relative. Therefore an answer related to this could also be:

> *'When someone dies, their body stops working and they become cold, as their breathing, blood and all the other things that go to make us alive are no longer working. But it sounds like you were able to say goodbye even if it was hard to understand that their body felt different. I hope that this helps as you get used to them no longer being here.'*

Question: 'What will happen to me?

Answers: Children who are from single-parent families, or from families who have separated, will have a particular need to know who will look after them now that their parent or carer has died. Sometimes parents and carers have made provision in a will for the possibility that they will not be able to look after their child, but often this is not the case as adults expect to be able to care for their child through to adulthood.

A child will therefore need to be told by a trusted adult (preferably within their family) who will be taking care of them when someone close has died. If this question is asked of professionals, it may be important for the professional to contact someone in the family (for example the ex-partner or a grandparent, if they know of one). Usually the person who brings a child to school will know the future plans. This information can then be conveyed gently to the child so that they have some knowledge of the changes they will experience.

Behind this question is the child's eternal need for safety and security. You can use some of the following examples and adapt them to the circumstances as appropriate:

> *'It has been really hard losing your [mum/dad/gran], and now you need to know where you will live and who will look after you. I am sure your [family/social worker] will be thinking very hard about what is best for you and they will also ask you what you want. Perhaps you are wondering if you can stay in your house. Would you like me to ask your [mum/dad/gran]?'*

Alternatively you could say:

> *'The most important thing to know is that whatever happens, you will be kept safe and continue to have a good life. You can tell me whenever you get upset about this, as changes like this are not easy.'*

Case study

Michelle was a very anxious 10-year-old who was very close to her mother. Her father, who had been separated from her mother for some years, had died a few months previously. Michelle was showing signs of withdrawal and was falling out with all of her friends. She also exhibited low self-esteem in all she did, even though she was quite intelligent. One day she asked a teacher: 'Did I cause my daddy's death? I can't ask mummy as she will be so cross with me.' During follow-on talks with her and through playing, it transpired that her last conversation with her dad had been on the phone, when she had been cross with him and told him she hated him. She had held this memory since his death and told no one as she had been so afraid that this had been the cause of his death. Explaining that he had been found to be very ill and had died rather suddenly helped her believe that it was not her fault. Her mum was informed of how Michelle had blamed herself and was also able to reassure her. Although she still needed to grieve fully, these conversations helped her to begin to make sense of her loss and not to blame herself. She began to emerge from her withdrawal and to play happily with her friends again.

Case study

Tom and Fiona were young children whose mum had been ill over a few months. Quite naturally, they found it hard to accept she was ill and often tried to make her do things like walk further than she was able, because they wanted her to be well. After a few months their mum became terminally ill and could not walk, so they spent all of their time in her bedroom. Eventually, she was moved to a hospice for treatment and then to die. At this point the family spoke more to the children, with the help of professionals, about what they wanted when mum died. They began to talk openly and their father prepared them for what mum might look like at death. Both children agreed they wanted to see her at death. After her death they spent a whole day by her side, and in fact were not frightened that she felt cold, could not walk, talk, and so on, as they had been told what to expect. They sat with her, told her things, gave her makeup and wrote her cards. In this way they made sense of her loss and later said how very important this time with mum after death had been to their acceptance that she was gone.

Questions about other losses

When loss occurs from other causes such as divorce, separation, moving home, military service and imprisonment, a child will still experience some of the same feelings as those felt around death and will have similar questions. A child may need reassurance that they are not to blame for the changes, may need to ask what will happen next for them and will continue to use their curiosity to try and adjust. Some of the following questions are typical of a child experiencing loss other than from death.

Question: 'Did I do something wrong?'

Answers: When a child asks this question, it is almost always because something has happened prior to the loss occurring. Younger children will naturally wonder if they are to blame for the changes, or for someone leaving the home. They will need to be reassured that it is not something they have done that has caused the change, and that the parent/carer left behind will continue to care for them in a normal, everyday way. Saying something like:

> *'No, you did not do anything wrong to cause this change. Your Mummy/Daddy and I decided that we could no longer live together although we still love you; your Mummy/ has had to go away for a while, but will still try and keep in touch by letter and phone.'*

This is a very direct response to the question, which may need answering a few times, as children tend to repeat the most difficult questions to make sure the answer remains the same. In addition they may need to know that you understand how difficult this is for them, with an empathetic response such as:

> *'I know how hard this is for you to understand and accept, and you can ask us whenever you need to, or come and tell us if and when you get upset about it.'*

This encourages a child to turn to an adult if they need extra support due to the loss. If appropriate you might also add:

> *'Even if you had an argument recently, or you were cross, it was not your fault, as nothing a child does like that is ever the reason for an adult going away/separating. Sometimes we just have to make difficult decisions, even ones that are hard for you.'*

This sort of response reassures a child that despite the (normal) behaviour of occasionally getting cross, having arguments, conflicts, this is not the reason for the changes. Again, it is normal for a child ask this sort of question a few times in order to check that it is really true that the loss is not their fault.

Question: 'What will happen to me?'

Answers: One of the significant things a child needs to know is what the plans are for their safe care when a change occurs due to a loss. When the loss is due to a separation, is it important to emphasise that you hope the child will stay in their usual home and see the person who is leaving as often as possible. It is not advisable to make promises you cannot keep, as children will remember these and lose some trust in adults if promises are broken. However, they will need to know that they are going to be looked after, who by, and where this will be if there is going to be a house move. With preparation, children can manage quite difficult losses such as separation and divorce well and continue to thrive. Examples of possible answers include:

> *'Well, we hope you can stay here in your home with me, and daddy/mummy will be moving somewhere else, but will keep on seeing you and being your daddy/mummy.'*

> *'We are going to move somewhere else, because I cannot afford to live here/we need to have a fresh start/Daddy [or Mummy] needs us to be near him/her. But it should be a good home just like this one, and I will continue to look after you.'*

> *'I know you are worried about what will happen and it is such a shock for you. But you must know that your family love you, and whatever happens you will be kept safe.'*

> *'I am so sorry you have had to go into foster care. But you know that the foster family will look after you well while your mummy/daddy tries to sort out what they need to have you back. You will still be able to see them [if this is true], as I know how important they are to you.'*

Adapt these suggestions according to the origin of the loss.

Question: 'Can I still see them?'

Answers: A child asking this question is asking for assurance that they can still have a daddy/ mummy/grandparent/carer that they care for. As the answer to this question will depend on the nature of the cause of loss, there are a number of possible responses. Included below are the most empathetic answers in situations of divorce/separation or when someone has been imprisoned or posted abroad on military service (which has its own strains). Use the following examples and adapt to the child's circumstances:

> *'We know how important it is for you that you keep in touch with [name of person] in some way, as we know how much you love them. However, sometimes when people separate/go away/move away it can be harder to do this. We will do as much as we can to make sure you can speak to them/write letters/contact each other over the computer/meet.'*

'Just because your mummy and daddy are no longer going to be living together, it does not mean you will not see them. They will do all they can to make sure you see them both regularly, perhaps staying over regularly once things are settled and choosing what is best for you. Many families change and separate, and most children seem to do fine with seeing their parents at different times. It may be hard, but they will do all they can to make it OK for you.'

Question: 'Why did you separate/choose a military job overseas/go to prison?'

Answers: This is the most difficult question for a child to ask and for adults to answer, as it makes you question your own decisions. However, be assured that children are asking this question mainly just to understand what has led to the experience of loss. Again children will need to be assured that the decisions made were not due to anything they have done wrong. They will need to know that the decisions are good and important ones for their family.

In the case of imprisonment, it may be important to decide what to tell a child, as some families will not want to tell very young children that a family member is in prison. However, it is normally advisable to tell them the truth, in simple terms, so that the child does not believe their relative has gone away because of something they have done. There are various different ways to answer this question, while remaining as honest as possible within the circumstances:

'Your parents chose to separate as they were unable to live together and do not love each other anymore. But they both love you and do not want any harm to come to you, so will try and do all they can to make sure you have as few changes as possible. It is sometimes really hard to explain to children how adults can decide not to live together any more as husband and wife, but it is definitely nothing that you have done.'

'Your [daddy/mummy] loves their job in the army/navy/RAF, and sometimes that means they have to go away and do their job abroad, protecting other people from harm. They are proud of their job and are very sorry that sometimes it means they have to be away from home. Try not to worry about what is happening to them while they are away. They will be able to contact you regularly, to keep in touch and to let you know how they are, so you will be able to tell them all your news. We will tell you when [he/she] is coming home.'

'Sometimes it is hard to explain why your [dad/mum] did something that ended up with them going to prison. But when someone does something against the law, sometimes the law says that person has to be punished by going away for a while. Your dad/mum will be able to write to you and, if your family want, you may be able to visit them. You can send them letters and cards, and some prisons have an arrangement where they can try and keep prisoners in close touch with their children, as they know how important it is. Even though it may feel like a long time, we hope that they will come home soon, so everything can get back to normal for you.'

Case study

Emily was 7 years old when her parents separated. Her mum chose to stay in the same house with her and her baby sister while her father left home. Emily was very worried at school and kept asking what was happening, why they needed to live apart and had great difficulty adjusting. She also spoke of her worries for her baby brother and did not want to be at school, because she said he was upset and crying all the time. School noticed she was more withdrawn and found it hard to say goodbye to her mum in the morning. They approached her mum to try and see what they could do together.

It transpired that it was taking a while to sort out somewhere suitable for her daddy to meet her, so she had not seen him for a few weeks and was becoming very upset about this. Emily's mother also agreed she was not having much luck getting extra support for the baby. School and mum worked together to help her find a place in a nursery for the baby. They also spoke to Emily about her dad still loving her, that he would come to see her very soon and that it was very important to him that he should see her because he loved her.

Although it had been a difficult separation, Emily's mum made more effort to tell her dad that he needed to meet with Emily soon, so he arranged to take her out weekly until his home situation improved. This helped Emily, who had begun to think it was something she had done that had caused the separation and her worries had been growing as a result. She was happy knowing her baby brother was at a nursery that he appeared to love. Once the arrangements were in place for her dad to meet with her weekly, and later to have her overnight, Emily's behaviour improved again, she appeared less distressed and she began to settle down.

Chapter 4
The Different Ways Children Express Loss & How to Support Them

It is the quality of our attention that allows us to be present with the mystery of death and suffering.

J.E. Roger, *The Art of Grief*, 2007

It is often very hard for adults to understand how children experience loss, and indeed if they grieve in the same way as adults. Seeing children very upset one minute, then happy and playing the next, can confuse us into thinking they are doing fine. One parent asks: 'How can he one minute seem upset that his daddy has died and the next minute run out to play with his toys?' However, children show their loss by dipping into and out of feelings continually as well as in myriad other ways, and it is not always obvious how a child is grieving. When younger, children often show their distress in physical symptoms such as stomach aches, headaches and feeling sick. Many parents are familiar with the confusion of hearing that a child feels sick and wondering if it is actually a physical sickness or a reaction to something stressful, for example at school or home.

As well as the descriptions given below of the ways in which children may respond to loss, there are practical suggestions for support that might be offered to alleviate distress in different situations, such as the classroom, the home and other environments.

When offering support to children who are responding to their grief or loss emotionally or physically:

- Choose the environment carefully, ensuring it is a safe, quiet place without bad associations for the child. This can be a library, head's office, corner of the classroom at school, or a quiet room if away from school.

- Check if the child wants to be alone with you or with another friend or adult.

👏 Ask gently if they would like to talk to you or someone else, or if they would prefer just to be quiet somewhere.

👏 Offer them a place to sit, such as a library or other quiet space, if they wish to be alone.

👏 Provide them with some art materials and books, toys (including puppets or dolls' house/pretend-play toys) and a pretend first-aid box if they would prefer to show you by this means how they feel.

👏 Remember to offer empathetic responses such as: 'It must be hard to have [reference to loss] happen to you', and 'I know you may not want to speak to anyone, and it is ok if that is what you want.' Key simple reflections that show you care are more important than finding solutions when children are experiencing loss.

This chapter is divided into various categories for ease of reference:

1   Physical reactions (mild), such as stomach aches, headaches, tiredness, nausea/sickness;

2   Physical reactions (severe), such persistent stomach aches, severe headaches/migraines, persistent nausea/sickness, inability to sleep/nightmares;

3   Emotional/psychological reactions (mild), such sadness/upset, anger, clinginess/insecurity, fears/anxieties, changes of personality & behaviour (e.g., from extrovert to introvert;

4   Emotional/psychological reactions (severe), such as relentless emotions/crying/anger, extreme withdrawal, changes of personality or behaviour; and

5   Difficult behaviours at school and home, such as school refusal, excessive anger, withdrawal (difficulty in playing/socialising), inability to concentrate, other strange behaviours.

Case studies are included to give examples based on real life and to show how children can be supported in a variety of situations; all of the details that might identify individuals have been changed.

1 Physical reactions to loss (mild)

Reacting physically is a normal expression of grief and loss. When a child complains of a pain in their body after something difficult has happened, this is a normal distress reaction. It is an expression of the pain that we all feel on experiencing loss, confusion or grief, and both adult and child will experience this. It can also be seen, in children, as a need for extra attention or comfort that will reassure them that their lives will be safe after the loss they have experienced. Mild physical reactions, though they can cause concern, are therefore not unusual. Examples of physical symptoms are shown below, with some support suggestions for how to respond to children who complain of these. Obviously it would be important to attend a GP clinic or other facility if a parent or carer is particularly worried: if, for example, persistent, extreme or prolonged pains exist.

Stomach aches

This is a typical reaction for younger children to loss and grief and, though distressing for parents and carers, is normally simply a way for a child to express their feelings physically. Children 'feel emotions' in their stomachs, and this pain (though very real to the child) should not truly be a cause for concern if it happens immediately after a loss, a death or a separation.

Support ideas

Sometimes offering a child a day or two off school when they complain of stomach aches can support their loss, though each family will have their own ideas of how important school is. However, often a stomach ache can be a child's way of asking to be closer to their carer at a significant time when they are experiencing normal feelings of insecurity. A child who has experienced loss, whether from bereavement, divorce/separation, or another cause, often needs reassurance and the security of knowing that the parent or carer who is in charge of them will not also leave them; the need to be close to the carer is often profound at this time. Most children who are bereaved take a few days off school, but not all children who experience loss such as separation or divorce do. If the stomach ache happens at school, try to gain the agreement of the family before offering to send them home.

Try to link their emotions to the pain, by saying such things as:

> *'I am sorry you are feeling a stomach/tummy ache. It may be that your pain is because you feel sad or upset/angry. You can always tell me if that is the case.'*

Or alternatively, if the adults around the child are also grieving or obviously upset:

> *'I wonder if your stomach is in pain just like I am in pain.'*

This may be true of grief from both bereavement and separation. It would then be appropriate, perhaps, for the adults to have a small conversation about what has happened, to check if this is why their stomach is hurting. A follow-on conversation could be:

> *'Let's think if your stomach is telling us something about your pain. Is there any way you can show me in your face how you feel?'*

Alternatively, as we know the child is finding it hard to speak directly about their emotional pain, it could be helpful to provide some drawing materials, ask them if they would like to draw a picture of how they feel and give them a quiet place to do this. If the child is at school, a teacher or school assistant could then sit with the child to see if they would like to tell them more about their drawing and their pain, or just to check if and when they are ready to return to class. Use one of the exercises in Chapter 6: A Toolkit of Activities, such as the 'Sad Self – Happy Self' worksheet, if necessary. At home the parent or carer could also check if the child is ready to talk or just needs to sit drawing quietly and choose when to go to their carer. Other professionals, such as social care professionals or health professionals, could similarly use these ideas to support the follow up of a stomach ache.

Headaches

This also is a typical reaction to loss, as a headache can literally mean a child is hurting in the head from what has happened. Obviously the sort of headache talked about here is not one of a migraine type, which lasts for days, but is the kind that simply comes and goes over a short period of time.

Support ideas

A child complaining of a headache is saying that their head is hurting, which could be directly related to their inability to make sense of the loss or death. For this reason ways of supporting that child would be connected to helping them understand what has happened. These can include asking them what they think has happened, helping them find a quiet space (whether at home, at school or another venue) so that there are fewer external stimuli to cause more pain, and finally helping them with empathetic support. Suggestions for what to say and do include:

'I am sorry you have a headache, do you want to tell me about it?'

'I wonder if your headache is so painful that you need to be somewhere very quiet to think quietly?'

'If you could draw your headache, what would it look like?'

After the last suggestion, you could discuss their drawing together with some more reflections about how hard it has been to experience their loss:

'Perhaps your headache is telling us that you don't know what has happened, do you have any questions to ask about ...?'

Make sure that you are not saying or asking these things in front of other children who are not supportive, or that you take the child to somewhere where they feel safe first. A child who has experienced loss automatically will feel less secure than usual.

Tiredness

Both adults and children experience tiredness as a result of loss and this is again a very normal and typical reaction. Children may find it hard to describe this, but can show listlessness or lack of concentration at school, or lack of interest in things they are normally interested in. They may not be sleeping well, or have other issues at night such as nightmares, which can add to the tiredness. If a child is falling asleep in the classroom this of course is a sign that they need more rest. Another way a child will show tiredness is by withdrawing from normal activities and isolating themselves.

Support ideas

When a child is showing signs of being tired, naturally they will actually need sleep. However the sort of tiredness that is caused by loss is a form of emotional fatigue. Therefore any form of empathetic response to do with their loss will help this particular reaction. This can simply be sympathetic comments, some actual reference to their loss, or a comforting hug if a carer is offering support. It can help to connect the physical tiredness to their feelings, saying such things as:

> *'I am really sorry you feel so tired. I wonder if it is anything to do with those things that have been happening to you recently?'*

> *'When someone feels tired, sometimes it means that inside there are lots of confused feelings going on; is that the case for you I wonder?'*

It may also be important for some children to not attend school for the whole day, as they may simply not have enough energy to manage this. Ask the children what they would like, and if they would prefer to take the occasional half day off. Not all children will want this, as some would definitely prefer to be with their friends (depending on their age), the details of the loss and what is happening at home.

Techniques to enable a child get to sleep at night can be helpful for children who are tired and struggling emotionally with their loss. Sometimes it is useful to read a relaxing bedtime story in a cosy way with their carer, to reassure them that they are safe and that sleep is possible. Sometimes it is possible to find a nice relaxing tape or CD for them to listen to, or even to use aromatherapy oils, which are an excellent way for a child to relax. Oils that are particularly relaxing include lavender, geranium and rose, which can all be put on an oil burner. Another way for children to relax is with a simple hand or foot massage. Children find this soothing and most parents can easily do this without training; it simply involves stroking the hand or foot gently. (See for example Atkinson 2009). Finally a hot, milky drink is often helpful in enabling a child to slowly relax, ready for sleep. Remember, however, that grief makes a person tired and sleep is only one aspect of the problem.

Nausea/sickness

Children can complain of feeling sick as a result of loss. Of course some children regularly complain of feeling sick and others never feel sick at all. But when a loss has affected them, this is a very normal reaction and one they share with adults. Again, it is the body saying that the child is feeling out of sorts and upset in ways they cannot fully describe, and it indicates that the grieving process is occurring.

Support ideas

As with stomach aches, feelings of sickness and nausea are often directly related to feelings of loss after a loss or bereavement has occurred. These feelings can be a child's way of expressing upset, sadness or anger indirectly. Helping them to link their feelings of sickness to their emotions can therefore help support them. It can also be important to offer comfort and support, as the sickness is also a call for care and attention at a difficult time.

Reflect on how hard it must be to feel a loss by saying, for example:

> *'It must be difficult to lose someone … and perhaps you feel sick as you are so upset and sad about this?'*

Offering empathetic support, whether as professional or carer, is usually important. Give the child time to rest, have cuddles and eat simple, comforting food. Obviously it will be important to rule out any physical cause for the sickness before making the connection between it and their loss. Since a child who feels sick may well feel poorly and tired also, it is probably best to keep a child off school for a short time, enabling some comfort from their carers, as well as allowing them to slowly recover.

Case study

Alan was age eight and had lost his grandfather, who was much loved, a few weeks before the summer term ended. He had attended the funeral and had been happy to go back to school immediately after his loss. However, his teachers noticed a tendency for him not to eat his lunch and not to go out to play in the week after the funeral. When asked about this, Alan could only say he had a tummy ache but would not talk about his grandfather. His parents were informed, and they were able to reassure him that the feeling in his tummy was about his upset feelings at losing his grandpa, and that it would pass. School helped by letting him go to a quiet corner when he needed to, and he was also encouraged to eat because he needed his strength to play. He began to show some normal feelings and cried a few times with his family. He also drew a picture of his grandfather and him playing, showing the significance of this relationship. Within a few weeks he was feeling much stronger and happier and, although his feelings continued to come out occasionally, he stopped complaining of his tummy ache and began to play normally with his friends again.

Case study

Jessica was a child of 10 years who had headaches after her aunt died suddenly. Jessica attended the funeral, but was unsure what had happened. She began to complain of headaches a few weeks later.

Her parents could not understand how to support her, as in other ways she appeared fine, not upset or withdrawn at all. When they went to the GP he suggested it might be related to her recent loss and suggested that they ask the school to keep an eye on her. School were informed and gave Jessica a time-out card (a discreet permission for the child to leave the classroom without having to ask each time: see the template in Resources), as well as the option to go and talk to a special teaching assistant whenever she felt the headache coming on. After using the time-out card twice, she admitted to the teaching assistant that she was confused about her aunt and wanted to talk to someone. She was worried about her cousins, the children of her aunt, but had not known what to say to anyone. She began to open up to the teaching assistant and agreed with her that her parents could be told about what she had said.

As a result of these actions her parents were able to help her understand why her aunt had died, that there was lots of support for her cousins, that she would still see them regularly and that everyone was upset by the aunt's death. She began to show her grief more appropriately after this and stopped having headaches almost immediately.

2 Physical reactions to loss (severe)

There are a number of factors that may influence a child to show more complicated responses to loss. These can include:

1   The causes of the loss, such as a suicide or a sudden accident which can be harder for a child to understand and respond to;

2   The nature of their relationship with the person they have lost, for instance a father they did not live with;

3   The experience of numerous losses, including divorce, other deaths, or changes of carers, all of which could compound the effect of loss;

4   Life in a household in which the grieving adults are too deeply immersed in their own grief to be available emotionally to their children;

5   Conversely, living in a household where the only one allowed to grieve properly is the child itself, with the adults focusing on the child in avoidance of their own grief;

6 An alteration to their life that stems from the loss, such as a change of school, home, carer;

7 A previous history of either mental or physical illness, which can compound a loss reaction.

All these factors can lead to a more complicated reaction physically to grief.

When a child reacts to loss with more compounded physical symptoms, this would normally indicate a deeper sense of loss and a more complicated way of responding that may take a little time to change. Although this can sometimes lead to a professional becoming involved, children can still be given excellent support by those around them and may not need this outside help. A more severe reaction that is shown physically, if there are no other indications of complexity, can simply indicate the depth of distress that needs to be acknowledged by those around the child. The general rule would be to define a severe reaction as one that seriously interferes with normal life.

Just a note of caution: most professionals who offer the sort of emotional bereavement support for children mentioned above make absolutely sure that both the children and related adults understand that this need to support is normally temporary and does not usually indicating an on-going need. Their aim is to avoid 'pathologising', that is to say treating the bereaved child's reaction as an illness and a disease rather than a temporary reaction to a difficult experience in life. Very few grief reactions lead to permanent illnesses.

Persistent stomach aches

If a child is constantly saying they have a stomach ache and is unable to eat, sleep or play as a result, there may be indications that another issue is involved rather than the actual stomach ache. Taking account of how long the child has complained of the stomach ache, how serious it appears to be and how it affects the child are all important. It is, of course, always advisable to rule out a physical cause first, by having a check-up with the local doctor. A teacher can talk to the parent to find out what else the child is saying or exhibiting, so that a clearer picture of what they may actually need can emerge. Sometimes persistent stomach aches can occur alongside other symptoms.

Support ideas

When a child has persistent painful stomach aches that are almost definitely as a result of emotional distress, the first priority is to help a child link the physical with the emotional pain. Offer empathetic responses, whether at home or at school, such as

> *'I am really sorry you feel such a pain in your stomach and I know how difficult life has been for you recently; it seems like your stomach is just showing the pain you feel inside.'*

Alternatively you could say:

> *'Perhaps your tummy pain is telling us how you feel upset and confused or sad about the recent loss you experienced?'*

If a child is not ready to respond to these comments, they will simply ignore them.

The next aspect of support that can be useful when a child is showing such symptoms is to help them express that pain. Therefore ask if they would like to show you the pain in a drawing or in play, always remembering to find a safe place, quiet and away from other children, unless they want a close friend nearby to help them. Giving a child something to do that is child-friendly, such as play in a doll's house or drawing, can really help a child find ways other than words to express how they feel, and this will hopefully reduce their need to have a serious stomach pain. If you are a professional and have some time to spare, sit with the child in a place where they are most comfortable and ask them if they can show you (using materials you have brought, such as drawing pens, paper, toys, puppets, soft toys, pretend first aid box) how they feel, because you would like to help their tummy ache. You may not have immediate reactions, but you should certainly help them in expressing the feelings that are causing the pains.

Finally, when a child has any pain (whether a stomach ache or serious headache) they are often in need of attention and reassurance. Therefore try to find someone who can give the child this attention for a short time (such as a teaching assistant), or check if the child is in need of their parent or carer if the pain persists. A child who has experienced loss will always be more insecure for a time and will need to know either that their carer is nearby, or to have the opportunity to speak or be with the carer more. This will then reassure them that life will get back to some kind of normality soon – and hopefully lessen the stomach ache.

Severe headaches/migraines

If a headache becomes so severe or so constant as to interfere with normal everyday activities, or is so painful that days in bed are needed, a child could normally be said to be showing a more severe reaction. This does depend on whether the child already has a history of such migraines and if they come on at certain times. Severe headaches that appear frequently and stop a child thinking, talking, playing or eating are likely to be emotionally related if the loss is serious and other physical causes are ruled out.

Support ideas

It is important for a child suffering from severe headaches or migraines that are presumed to be as a result of loss to feel supported.

Occasionally a child will describe having a pain in the part of the body where the person who has died was ill and this can usually be talked through with the child to reassure them that they will not become ill in the same way. You could say, for example:

> *'You know [name of person] had an illness in their head and I wonder if your own pains are sort of because you are worried you will get ill in the same way, or because you can't stop thinking about them? Let's see if we can reduce your pain by helping you understand that your pain is to do with how you feel. What [name of person] had was caused by [illness/accident/other]. You aren't going to be sick in the same way, though it must feel very hard for you.'*

In having the sort of pain that stops a child doing anything, they are saying that they cannot cope with their loss without lots of time to recover. Therefore offering a child a short time away from school, some comfort time with their carers/parents, and some enjoyable quiet time at home with few challenges and stresses can begin to address this sort of pain. Some of the feelings exercises later in this book (Chapter 6: A Toolkit of Activities, Exercises for Working with Specific Feelings) can also be very helpful, since they may help children to begin to connect their physical pain to their emotional pain. It can simply sometimes need an empathetic comment or two from adults, such as:

> *'It must be so hard to feel that pain in your head and perhaps it is to do with all the horrible things that have been happening to you lately? Would you like to talk about this or even do something else to do with how you feel and what you are thinking?'*

> *'I wonder if that big pain in your head means you need to spend a bit more time at home getting used to all the things that have happened? Then the painkillers and the talking can do their work to help.'*

Persistent nausea/sickness

This should also be seen as more severe if the complaint of feeling sick is made constantly and regularly, has happened over a prolonged period of time and affects most mealtimes. As a result of this reaction, the everyday need to eat will be affected, one of the signs that the physical reaction is more severe.

A child who is constantly feeling sick and nauseous is showing their feelings in this reaction, and once a visit to the GP has ruled out a physical cause it can be presumed that the cause is emotional distress in reaction to their loss.

Support ideas

Within school, it will be important for professionals to be in touch with the child's family so that both family and school can work together to support a child. This is particularly so as they may be refusing to eat or drink, or may be physically sick on school premises. An agreement can be made for a family member to be called or to come into school if a child becomes so severely sick that they cannot return to class. However, it can also be helpful for a child to see that both family and school together care about how they are and wish to support them.

Parents and carers can offer support by trying not to make a large event of mealtimes, by lessening the attention a child gets as a result of being sick and by trying to allow the child to link how they feel to their physical reactions. Food in particular is a very emotive area for children and carers, and can occasionally become a battlefield. Therefore, although parents should offer support and care to a child who is sick and nauseous and perhaps refusing food, they should also remember the guideline of giving attention to positive behaviour not negative behaviour. If necessary allow a child to sit at a table and not eat, or not attend a mealtime, or give them another activity during mealtime, while saying to them that you need them to eat regularly so that they stay healthy. Remember in particular not to allow an argument over food and mealtimes; always make it a positive, routine event, while making it clear that the child is temporarily not able to eat as they feel sick.

By not giving attention to the negative behaviour, though offering care and support by saying that you really do not like them to be sick, you are allowing the child to have some attention, but transferring it as smoothly as you can to the emotional cause rather than the food and sickness, which is their way of showing the pain. Using some of the previous exercises to help a child link the pain to their feelings is vital in helping them to find new ways to express their feelings, while also asking them if there is anything they particularly need to tell you.

Your comments on the situation could include:

> *'It seems your tummy just won't accept food at the moment; I wonder if that means you are so upset you need a rest from anything else?'*

> *'It must be so hard to feel sick all the time. Sometimes, when someone is sick like you are, the feelings inside your stomach have become so stuck that they have nowhere else to go but into the sick feeling. I wonder if we can find some way to help unstick these feelings, as it is important for you to start eating again soon? If you do not eat you will not be able to grow strong and healthy and do all the things children love to do.'*

> *'Although we understand how hard it is for you to eat, I wonder if we can decide together what sort of things you can eat, so we keep you safe and well? Perhaps you would like to speak to someone about how you feel while this is going on, so that you know we are listening to you?'*

Professionals supporting such children may need to keep in contact with parents to ensure that there is a joint strategy. Teaching assistants can then be available to sit with a child during mealtimes, to encourage them to eat if possible, but also to hear them and play or draw with them if this is what they prefer to do. Leave the child the option to eat or not a few times, but you could also say, for example:

> *'Normally we would expect you to attend meals and eat lunch like everyone else, but we understand that at the moment you are particularly upset about your loss so we are giving you some time to get used to this.'*

This both reinforces the normal rules of behaviour over food and also allows them to link feelings to their physical reactions.

Inability to sleep/nightmares

Although many professionals may not actually know if a child is not sleeping, it will normally be observable in a classroom or elsewhere, for example by a child being listless or lacking in concentration. Lack of sleep can be caused by many things and can also lead to many different behaviours. These include changes in normal behaviour, isolation, irritation, excessive quietness and inability to concentrate, amongst others. When this is a constant and continual problem it may indicate many things, of course, but in relation to loss and grief it can certainly indicate a more complicated reaction to a loss.

Support ideas

As with all other more complicated reactions, turning to the family first for their understanding of what is happening to their child is important and valuable. A teacher would then contact the main family carer to discuss what is happening at home, and specifically at night, and together they would decide if the lack of sleep is serious enough to think of going to a GP or allowing the child to take some time off school. There are sometimes things happening in the home that a carer has forgotten to mention to school, but which are affecting a child, for example: a new member of a family coming to stay; a new room or roommate; a different babysitter; or other changes affecting night-time. School and family together should be able to decide if any of these factors are affecting the child.

Once that has been clarified, the next step would be to discuss why this might be happening and to examine other support measures, such as helping the family to find ways of enabling the child to sleep. The previous suggestions regarding aids to sleep, such as a cosy bed-time story with a carer and oils to fill the room with good smells, can be helpful. If nightmares are an issue, it is vital to reassure the child that everyone has bad dreams sometimes, perhaps suggesting that child and carer could chase them away together by drawing or talking. Just raising the fact that a child is clearly not able to enjoy school as a result of their nightmares or lack of sleep will enable a parent to give more attention to the child's experience of loss. Just as professionals find it hard to know how to support children in loss, so do parents sometimes and encouragement can help all adults to acknowledge how hard it is for children to actually say what they need.

Examples of what to say include:

> *'I am really sorry you are not sleeping well and having bad dreams. That must be really bad and is making you tired and grumpy. Make sure you tell your parent, so that they can comfort you when it happens. At [school/other environment] we can help by giving you time to relax in a corner on a cushion when you get too tired to do the work. Or we can ask for your parents to come and pick you up if you are really too tired to stay here. What would you prefer?'*

> *'When children have bad dreams and nightmares, we usually say to them that it is important to tell someone what it is you are dreaming so that they can help you chase it away. It is horrible to wake up scared, and I hope you know you can tell us whenever you do.'*

Parents need to remember always to reassure children who wake up scared and frightened as it is one of the worst experiences of childhood to wake up after a bad dream. Comfort, cuddles, reassuring drinks, going into a parent's bed, putting on a night light and holding a special toy can all help. A reassuring comment might be:

> *'Remember to wake me up and tell me if you are ever too scared to sleep because of bad dreams. I will help you feel safe as that is my job. I am so sorry that because of the recent things that have been happening you are having these nightmares. I can help you if you tell me.'*

Case study

Sarah, age 7, lived with her grandmother and regarded her as a second mother. It was therefore a great shock when her grandmother died of cancer at only 58. She appeared to understand that her granny was not coming back and attended the funeral, but naturally began to have mood swings after her loss. She then went off her food and stopped eating for over two weeks. Doctors could not find any physical cause for this, but she continued to refuse all solid food and began to lose weight, although she continued to have milky and other drinks, so was not regarded as seriously at risk. Her school was informed and they attempted to ensure she ate school meals, which she nearly always refused. She was monitored throughout by health professionals.

During discussions with her parents, it transpired that Sarah had seen her beloved grandmother feeling nauseous, being sick and refusing food. There appeared to be some connection. Sarah had believed that by being sick herself she could remain close to her granny and so remained in a stage of denial. This is a normal stage of grief in both children and adults, and Sarah believed that if she did not eat she would both stay close to her granny and possibly bring her back. As she was still of the 'magical thinking' age, during which children believe their actions can affect things such as life and death, this was a logical reaction to her loss that no one had previously understood.

By spending some time with a professional, Sarah began to understand the permanence of death, to connect her refusal to eat with her deep distress at losing her granny, and was eventually able to eat solids again when her emotions found more natural outlets. She returned to being a normal, happy, more confident child within two months, though still very sad and upset at her loss in a more appropriate way.

Case study

Tom was 11 and began to have severe migraines about once a fortnight three months after losing his dad. His dad (a teacher) had been knocked down on his bike on the way to school and lay in a coma for three days before he finally died. Tom learnt about the accident only when he returned from school himself the same day. It was a shocking loss for Tom, his mum and his sister. But Tom was apparently particularly affected, though he had shown no other signs of grief and was apparently 'normal' at school.

After taking him to the GP and having tests done that showed no physical problems, his mum agreed it could be related to their loss. The family were all very sad and angry, but she noted that she and the sister naturally cried and talked about the father all the time, whereas Tom did not like to talk about him and ran from the room when they started to cry. There was to be a court case and they were not looking forward to it.

The school offered Tom a counsellor, but he refused. However, he did agree to talk to a teaching assistant who he trusted and liked. During the course of this talk, he did a drawing of his dad in the hospital; the assistant was shocked when Tom told him that this was only the way he could now remember his dad. Because this was the only picture of his father in his head, he had developed the headaches that hurt his head so badly. He admitted that he could not understand why his dad had been allowed to die. He was very angry with the driver of the car, at his dad for not taking more care, and with himself for not being able to see him sooner. He had seen his dad in the hospital wired up to all the monitors and had understood that he was still alive then. Tom's brain had simply not accepted that later his father had died. It was too shocking for him.

The teaching assistant spoke to the school counsellor, who considered that Tom was in shock as a result of the suddenness of the loss followed by seeing his dad in a very alien place in hospital, and that this had given him some of the symptoms of post-traumatic stress disorder. He was literally frozen at the point in which his dad lay in a coma, not accepting that he had died after this.

Tom therefore agreed to meet with the counsellor, providing that the teaching assistant was there for some of the time. He needed someone with whom he felt safe to begin the counselling sessions. The counselling helped him to unfreeze his grief and release the memory that had become stuck in his brain, which helped his migraines. Within two months he was able to begin to cry, although he was in severe emotional pain; he also began to show signs of anger, a healthier reaction to a very difficult experience. His family agreed to be less open about their crying until he was able to begin his own adjustment.

3 Emotional/psychological reactions (mild)

Children will naturally show upset and distressed feelings when they lose a person close to them. This is quite normal and is exactly the same reaction as experienced by adults. Sadness, anger, fear, worry, confusion and withdrawal are common, and with most children these reactions will be temporary and short-lived, as children like to dip in and out of feelings even when a serious loss has occurred.

Remember these key points when you are about to talk to a child suffering from emotional or psychological reactions to loss: prepare the environment in advance; consider carefully what might be said to a child under the circumstances; have useful materials available; and never shame a child by talking in front of others unless they are good friends that the child wants near. The following are a small selection of ways in which a child will respond emotionally or psychologically, as well as some support ideas.

Sadness/upset

Children will quite naturally feel sad and upset when they are beginning to grieve for a loss. This sadness may come and go; they can seem perfectly happy one minute, and deeply distressed the next. This is a quite normal way of coping with the unusual feelings associated with loss. A child may cry for a short time, perhaps at night, or in a playground for a minute, then return to playing and acting more normally. However, they will need reassurance that their feelings are normal when experiencing a loss. They will also need some help in finding ways to express these feelings safely.

Support ideas

Families usually grieve together when someone has died, or they have experienced a loss. Being sad together is good for a child, as it encourages them to be open about their feelings if the adults nearby are also open appropriately. If an adult is crying all the time, however, this can be less helpful as the adult's grief can sometimes swamp the child's need to grieve. Families have a tendency to protect each other, and children will want to protect their adults just as the adults wish to protect them. Therefore it can be helpful for the adults to monitor how much of the feelings of sadness and upset they show, but not to avoid them. In this way they can support each other while still expressing feelings. Examples of what to say include:

> *'I am really sorry you are feeling so sad/upset. It is normal to feel this way when someone dies/you have experienced a separation [etc.] Please tell me when you feel sad so that I can comfort you/give you a cuddle.'*

> *'I guess it is hard to feel sad sometimes when all your friends are out having fun. Remember it is OK to have fun too; just because you have lost someone does not mean you cannot be happy some of the time.'*

If a child is crying a lot at school and needing some extra attention, it is often useful to have an arrangement whereby a child can use a time-out card (a discreet permission for the child to leave the classroom without having to ask, see the template in Resources), or another technique to show they need a bit of extra support. This can be used for them to go and sit somewhere safe, or to meet with someone to have a chat, or just to be quiet for a short while. Since children dip into and out of feelings associated with loss, most of the time children will be able to return to a class quite quickly.

Remember to make empathetic reflections rather than trying to make everything better, as pain from loss cannot be easily removed. Examples of what to say include:

> *'It feels like you are so sad at the moment, because of what has happened. I am really sorry you feel like this. Let me know whenever you need time just to sit or draw.'*

> *'When you feel sad, the world feels an upside-down sort of place. Would you like to draw or show me what that feels like, to help that sadness come out so you can be happy again at some point?'*

Anger

Similar to the sad feelings, children who have experienced loss can become angry, a normal feeling associated with grief and loss. This anger can take many forms, including being cross at something which would normally be easily accepted, or being a bit more cross or irritable than usual with their friends or family. Generally there is nothing to be concerned about, though it is usually helpful to remind the child, and even their friends, that as a result of their loss these feelings may be present more and are natural. If children are given a safe outlet to express anger, such as during sports, telling stories or playing, the anger will not usually become more severe. Children simply need to be reassured that what they are feeling is fine and there is nothing wrong with them.

Support ideas

As anger is not often an acceptable feeling either at home or at school, it can sometimes be hard for a child to know how to express this safely and appropriately. They will also need to know that there is nothing wrong with them for having these feelings as a result of a loss. Therefore giving a child ways in which to express their anger safely is vital. Have art materials, play materials and even a drum on hand to offer them a chance to be angry safely. Offering a child a time-out card (a discreet permission to leave the classroom without asking) so that they begin to recognise when they need time out of the class at school to 'cool down' is often useful for children who may become more out of control than usual. Direct them to a place where they can be safe, quieter, or able to do an activity that will help them with their feelings while giving some attention to their loss. Behind most feelings of anger associated with loss is deep grief and mourning. Examples of what to say and do include:

> *'It seems like you are getting more angry than usual and that is normal when someone loses someone like you have. Would you like to show me [using drawings, toys, and so on] what that looks like?'*

> *'I know being angry is not normally what you do. But don't worry, most children get angry when something horrible happens like a person dies/parents separate.'*

> *'I wonder if you know that being angry is OK, but it is not OK to take it out on other people or things. Can you think of any ways to be angry safely? Or ways to show me that you are angry without getting into trouble?'*

If a child needs help with calming down as a result of becoming angry more quickly than usual, try using the breathing exercises often used in anger management (Chapter 6: A Toolkit of Activities, see Activity 9 'Calming Breaths'). Ask the child to count to ten. Get them to hold their breath while doing this, so they should not count too slowly. Then ask them to slowly count backwards from ten to one, releasing their breath and with it some of the anger. By the time they get to one they should be calmer. This can be done two or three times if needed, but no more as the child could hyperventilate. Most children enjoy this exercise and recognise that as a result of this they can begin to have some control over their feelings. This is helpful for children who have experienced loss, as their life may feel out of control more than usual.

Clinginess/insecurity

As a result of loss children quite naturally will feel less secure in their world, as someone to whom they were close and who helped them feel safe has gone. This is true whether the lost person was a parent, a sibling or close grandparent and it is also true no matter what the cause of the loss. Therefore children are often clingy and more insecure for a time after a loss. This is a natural response for a child, particularly one who has not previously experienced much change in their lives. With reassurance from the adults who care for them, and perhaps some extra patience, most children who do show clingy behaviour (for instance at the school gates) can soon return to a more confident separation.

Support ideas

You could use one or a combination of the following ideas:

- Reassure a child who is insecure that nothing is going to happen to you as a parent while they are at school. Sometimes children who have experienced loss from death, in particular, worry that the parent left behind will also die, so this reassurance can be vital to help them feel safe again.

- Allow a child more time to say goodbye at the school gates, or go into the school classroom if necessary to help the transition between home and school.

- Give them time to show their feelings when saying goodbye, then establish the normal routine of saying goodbye and assuring them you will be there to see them at the end of the day.

- Give them something to take into school, such as a small toy which will not get lost or something that they can touch and hold in their pocket. This can be very reassuring as it is something from home and will act as a kind of 'security blanket', enabling a child to begin to feel safe away from the home after a significant loss. Always tell the teachers you have given your child such an item, as it is not a good idea for the child to lose it.

- Professionals, including teachers, can make an arrangement with a parent that they will be present at the beginning and end of the day, to 'hand over' the child with the minimum of fuss. A child needs to be reassured that some things remain the same, although their feelings of insecurity are causing them to question whether or not a situation really is safe. A teacher (or even an older child) offering to take a child to their seat, or having a book on hand to show the child, can be very valuable to a child who is showing signs of insecurity.

Occasionally, a child showing signs of insecurity will need a little longer off school, to feel safe within their home environment and with their family before returning to school. This can be negotiated between school and family. Examples of what to say include:

'I am really sorry it is hard for you to say goodbye to mummy today. Here is your teacher who is going to show you something to help you feel good about being here.'

'I will give you three extra cuddles before we say goodbye. Then I can do the same when we meet at the end of the day. How does that sound?'

'It feels so hard to say goodbye, but you know I am not going to go anywhere, I will be at home/work/other and school can always get hold of me if you need me. I will be here at the end of the day as normal.'

'Here is your toy/object to take into school with you. Whenever you feel a bit unsafe, you can get it out and hold it so it reminds you of me and home. Your teacher knows about it.'

Fears/anxieties

In a similar way to clinginess, children quite naturally can have fears associated with their loss. They may, for example, have nightmares or seem withdrawn as a way of showing these fears. A particular fear is often that their remaining parent, if it is a parent who has died, will also die. Another fear that a child can often have is that in some way they caused the death if the loss they are suffering is from death. This is also true for those children who experience separation or divorce and who can believe they are to blame in some way. Being reassured that these fears are simply fears and not real, can usually help.

Support ideas

Telling a child clearly what is happening and when, who will be looking after them, that they will not be moving home, and so forth, is the most important way of alleviating fears at times of loss. If they are afraid that their surviving parent will die/move etc., they will need to be reassured that this will not happen and that life will continue as normally as possible.

Sometimes the fears and anxieties are directly related to the specifics of the loss, or to things they have overheard. It usually helps, therefore, to encourage a child to share their fears. If a child is not willing to tell their parents or carers, they may be willing to tell another trusted adult. They may also start by telling their pet or their toys first, which is quite normal. A fearful child, who is also fearful of getting into trouble and of what may happen if they speak to an adult, may need to practise first with toys and pets. Examples of things to say include:

'Whatever you have heard, we need to know if you are scared of certain things happening or believe things will be even more horrible. You have had such a difficult time I would want you to feel happy and secure again now.'

'Would you like to tell me or another adult what is troubling you? It is clear you have some worries and fears, but it seems hard to tell someone. If you don't want to tell a person, would you want to tell your pet, or a toy?'

'When someone has worries, it often is best to tell someone. If not, those fears and worries become bigger and bigger, until they have to come out and be told – let's have a look at the Big Bag of Worries *book if you don't believe me [see Chapter 7: Resources, Suggestions for Further Reading]. Do you think your worries and fears are ready to come out and be shared?'*

Changes of personality and behaviour (e.g., from extrovert to introvert)

Quite often when a child first loses someone they love, they will respond in chaotic ways that are not typical of their normal personality. They may therefore become more quiet or withdrawn and play less with their friends. Alternatively, they may also become more animated, over excitable and extrovert. This again could be seen as a generally normal reaction to loss, particularly if this is a small, temporary change. Both adults and children take time to adjust to loss, and this is one way in which the disorientation that is felt when a loved one dies or a parent leaves after a divorce can show itself.

Support ideas

When a child changes personality or becomes less predictable, it can be quite shocking for those around them. However, this is simply the child reacting to their loss appropriately. Being honest with them about how strange it is to see them quiet, or loud, crazy or mad, allows the child to know you have noticed their reaction and hope to support them in their loss. Again, it is important to link their behaviour to their feelings so that they can begin to adjust to their loss. It may also be important that their reactions are noted, as this is a sign either that they would like more attention, or that they do not want any attention depending on their introvert/extrovert reactions. For a child who has changed to withdrawn, it could be helpful to say, for example:

'I notice you have become very quiet, and wonder what you need to tell me about that? Perhaps it is something to do with how you feel about your recent loss?'

'I wonder, as you are not saying much, if it's hard for you to know what to say? Perhaps you would like to show me in other ways [e.g. drawing, play] as we really want to know what is going on to support you.'

For children who have had the opposite reaction, becoming more extrovert, excitable or even angry, examples of what to say include:

'I have noticed that you are much louder at the moment. Perhaps you want to be noticed and have your say about how you feel – maybe it's to do with the loss you recently experienced, what do you think?'

'It feels really important to listen to some of the things you are saying, but I also notice that sometimes you make a big fuss of something – do you think you are trying to tell us something, perhaps about how you find it hard to manage at the moment? Perhaps you would like to show me with art/toys/etc.?'

Case study

Ruth was a sophisticated 10-year-old who had known for two years that her mother was seriously ill. When her mum finally died, she was quite naturally distraught and began to show changes of behaviour. She found it hard to sleep at first and became very quiet at school. In other ways she appeared fine. Following discussions with her father and grandparents, they realised that she found it hard to speak to her friends about all she had experienced and that she had become anxious about school playtime. She felt different from the other children as she no longer had a mother, and her feelings and experiences of the last two years had made her feel older. She was therefore helped by her teachers to speak with her friends, who reassured Ruth that she was still one of them and helped to integrate her back into the normal life of school. The family had made sure that as little as possible changed for her when her mum died and this also helped her to feel less insecure.

Case study

Jack was 6 years old when his dad moved away. His mum and dad had explained everything that was going to happen and had tried to prepare him for the changes when his dad was no longer in the house. However, Jack found it hard to adjust and a year later appeared to have changed from a normal, well-adjusted child to an angry, almost out-of-control one. He showed this more at school than at home, therefore his parents were very surprised when school contacted them to talk about his behaviour. He had been getting into fights and shouting more at other children.

School had tried to talk to him to find out if there was anything in particular that was bothering him, but he did not seem to know. When they spoke to mum, she wondered if it was a delayed reaction to their divorce. Mum therefore took sometime over the following week to spend extra time with him. During this he admitted that he hated having his dad live away from the home and that, even though their weekends were fun, it was not the same. Then he admitted something new: that his dad had begun to have a girlfriend visiting when he was there. This is what had upset him.

As a result of this talk, his mum contacted his dad and they discussed the issue of the girlfriend and Jack's reaction to this. They realised that Jack was more sensitive than they had thought, and that his dad would have to be more careful, introducing new ideas and new changes carefully. This was one new change he was not ready for. Luckily his dad cared for Jack so much that he changed his arrangements: he agreed that he would not meet up with his girlfriend while Jack was staying with him until everyone was sure that Jack had had sufficient time to prepare for a new person in his family.

After these talks Jack's behaviour changed considerably: he became less angry and he began to settle to school again. He still had some potential to become angry faster, and for this he was given a bit of extra support by a teaching assistant who offered some of the exercises found in Chapter 6: A Toolkit of Activities. Jack settled down far more and became a happy child again, generally well adjusted.

4 Emotional/psychological reactions (severe)

Sometimes children have more complex reactions to their loss. This can be because of a previously complicated family history, or because of something they have seen or experienced that has affected them more profoundly. Because losing a parent or loved one (for whatever reason) is a trauma in itself, other factors such as previous separation or losses of different nature can sometimes cause a more severe reaction. In these cases a professional can be useful in providing help that allows the child to adjust to their loss. Again, the aim of any professional is not to 'pathologise', but to help the child adjust to a particular life experience. In some cases teachers can certainly act as these professionals.

Relentless emotions/crying/anger

Sometimes children show their feelings of loss by crying all the time, being angry all the time, or being fixed in one state of emotion that they cannot control at all. This could be described as a complex reaction, because it would stop them from experiencing their normal routine. Such a child may sit in a corner, red-eyed, for days, not do their work at all, need to leave the classroom every hour, or be forever in trouble for being angry in the classroom to the extent that they are always fighting, shouting, perhaps even throwing furniture around. This is normally a sign that the grief is either complex or stuck at a certain stage, and speaking to carers (or to the child themselves) may begin to address this. If this continues for longer than perhaps a month or two, it may then be important to speak with a child's family and explore how to support the child to help their grief.

Support ideas

For children who show more complex emotional and psychological reactions, such as extreme sadness or anger, it may be that mental health professionals can help alongside your support. However, before bringing in other professionals consider trying the following techniques:

- Give the child a time-out card, which allows them to choose when they are ready to leave the classroom if they feel upset or sad without having to ask each time. Ensure that the place where they go is one where they feel very safe and where an adult they can trust is present. This gives them space away from their feelings and allows them to begin to return to being in control.

- Ask the child who they would turn to if they needed extra support, then arrange for this person to be available regularly for emotional support when the child cries or becomes extremely angry again.

- Reflect regularly on how hard it is for them to be sad or angry at school so that they know someone has recognised their distress.

- Allow the child to bring in a much-loved toy to comfort them whenever they need this.

Examples of things to say include:

> *'It must be very hard to be sad/angry/upset all the time. You have had a difficult time recently and I wonder if you would like to speak to someone about this?'*

> *'I wonder if your feelings of sadness/anger are telling us that the things that have happened recently to you and your family are too hard to bear? Shall we ask your mum/ dad about this, to see if they can help you sort it out?'*

Ask the family if anything has occurred in the family home. Sometimes when a child is showing emotion continuously, there are other factors at play that even the family have not connected to this reaction. For example, another loss that they have not registered as important, but which has affected the child. Reactions such as this to loss normally indicate a complicated grief reaction due to more than one cause: perhaps multiple losses, a complicated emotional history with the person they have lost, or a significant memory that has blocked other grief reactions.

Try looking at Activities 4–12, Exercises for Working with Specific Feelings (Chapter 6: A Toolkit of Activities) to see if these might be helpful, since these enable a child to explore their deeper feelings safely. Remember the guidelines for ensuring that the child feels secure in their environment if you are using these exercises, particularly if a child is very vulnerable.

Extreme withdrawal

Children may also show their feelings of loss by being very, very quiet and withdrawn (so that no one is able to talk to them at all for days) and by being unable to concentrate or say what they want. It can be very sad to see children in such a state of being, and the adults who do see this would normally be advised to speak to the child's carers, to try to find some way of engaging with the child if possible, or to check who the child feels they can talk to. Such a child often has many worries they are not sharing with anyone, perhaps because they do not want to cause trouble or are not sure what to say and who to say it to. It is also true that these children are sometimes overlooked; rather than drawing attention to themselves, they are sometimes almost invisible, particularly in a busy classroom.

Support ideas

For such children it is important not to draw attention to them unnecessarily, but to try and offer support discreetly. For example:

- Ensure that there is someone they can talk to or turn to, if needed, at lunchtime or playtimes when children who are withdrawn have most difficulty.

- See if there is an ally in one of their peers, as children acting like this often have few friends or feel very low self-esteem, therefore do not naturally reach out to others. A peer-support system in some schools helps with this sort of child who will never ask for support obviously.

- Peer-support networks work by training children who are interested in some of the very basic skills of counselling and care. They are taught to show empathy in particular and to be available if needed.

- If the parents are not aware that their child is like this at school, it can be very useful for schools to make contact and speak to them. Discussions between families and schools can always be helpful for children who are not thriving at school so that teachers know the home situation.

Examples of what to say include:

> *'I wonder if you are feeling quiet for a special reason? I know you don't want to draw attention to yourself, but it might help to tell someone how you are feeling, to help you.'*

> *'Is there a safe place in school you would like to go when you feel particularly quiet? A school is a busy place sometimes for someone who has had the sorts of troubles you have had, and maybe being somewhere quiet with someone you trust will feel easier?'*

Case study

Daniel was 9 years old when he lost his much-loved father who had been depressed and had taken an overdose. Daniel's mother was grief-stricken and had therefore found it very hard to support him as well as herself. He was becoming obsessive about cleanliness and would not play for fear of making a mess. In addition, he was beginning to have what could only be called severe tantrums, despite being 9 years old, and these were seen as out of character. His tantrums would regularly turn physical, with him hitting out at other children and banging his head against walls. At home he was said to just sit quietly and play on the computer.

With the help of an external professional and school staff, Daniel was able to begin to make sense of his loss, to talk about what had happened and to begin to allow his feelings of deep grief and shock out more appropriately. His loss had been very traumatic and unexpected, and he needed to understand that he was not to blame and was not the only child to lose a loved father to suicide. He attended a group particularly for children bereaved by suicide and was able to begin to play again, to become less obsessed with cleanliness (an obsession he shared with his father), and to enjoy his life once more. His mother also gained her own support and kept in touch with school staff so that Daniel could feel supported both at home and school.

5 Difficult behaviours at school and home

Often, when children are grieving, the only way in which adults close to them know that something is wrong is when it is obvious from their behaviour. Children's natural form of communication, especially in their younger years, is through play and behaviour. Therefore, observing the behaviour of children who have experienced loss can be an indication of how well they are coping. Some behaviours have already been mentioned, but there are a variety of behavioural patterns with which it can be helpful to be familiar if you are unsure that the child's behaviour is an sign of need.

School refusal

Children may sometimes refuse to go to school. This can be for many reasons, but the prime reason for children who have experienced loss is that they feel scared and insecure, because they have lost someone close to them. When a child has lost one adult, or a sibling, they are always afraid that someone else in the family will also die. Being reassured can help with this, and making a school professional available to provide support can also help.

Support ideas

Giving a child some way of communicating with a parent in the early days of the loss, perhaps via a mobile phone, is often extremely valuable for extra reassurance. Some schools will allow this, and others may ask that a child request a phone call via the school office. Simply knowing that they can contact their carer at any point in the day can help avoid more school refusal.

The balance between making sure a child goes to school and allowing their feelings of loss and grief is a delicate one. When a child refuses to go to school, balance has not been found, therefore it is usually helpful for the child to have some other ways to feel more secure. They may also need to know that any acceptance that they do not need to attend school on some days is only temporary, because their carers and the school want to support them. You could say, for example:

> *'We understand that you find it hard to go to school at the moment as you have had some difficult experiences of loss. But we will have to decide together how to help you and when you will return. You will miss out on so much if you don't go back soon.'*

When such children are at home, it is helpful for them to spend good, quality time with their carers or parents, trying to find out how they are, whether they are expressing simply a need to be at home safe for a short while, or whether they have more hidden, complicated feelings that they need help with. A parent could say, for example:

> *'I am glad you are at home today, though of course you should not normally miss school. Perhaps we can do something really special together today, then tomorrow we can check out if you have any questions or want to tell me more about why you don't want to go?'*

Excessively angry behaviour

Children may show extremes of behaviours such as having angry outbursts. They can call extra attention to themselves in this way, for instance by having more fights, or being disruptive and rude. Children can have great difficulty understanding their feelings and their loss, including how they feel about death. This then leads them to have no way to express their loss other than by demanding attention. They often do not understand why they have done this, however. They may not make a connection between their behaviour and their experience of loss. Therefore, helping them to connect their behaviour to their feelings of loss can often be more helpful than asking them why they are behaving as they are or asking them to stop it.

Support ideas

Children who are showing signs of excess anger may need an outlet for their anger at the same time as help to link their behaviours to their feelings. Discipline is important, but also it can be important to emphasise that feeling anger is normal and acceptable, although the manner in which they are expressing it at the moment (destructive, antagonistic) is not. Examples of what to say and do include:

> *'We know how you are having difficulty with your anger at the moment, as you seem to want to take it out on other people and things. I wonder if this is to do with the recent losses you have experienced? If this is the case, maybe you would like to show me how you really feel [by drawing or playing with toys], because taking you anger out in this way is not acceptable.'*

> *'I wonder if one of the reasons you are getting angry a lot is because of what you have experienced and you want me to notice you. I am noticing you, but I am also concerned and wonder if you really feel upset and don't really know what to do about it. That is OK, as people who experience what you have experienced often get upset. Perhaps we can find safer ways together to express your feelings, and maybe you would like to speak to someone about this?'*

Remember to acknowledge the feeling and to empathise with the child's pain, while also continuing to remind them of the discipline and boundary needs around a child who becomes very angry. At some point you will need to ask them to choose between a more normal behaviour and this unacceptable behaviour. But in the short term, if the unacceptable behaviour is connected to loss, allowing them to hear that you empathise with their feelings gives them a better chance of calming down. Use some of the previous exercises on anger management (see the notes under mild emotional/psychological reactions, above) to help a child to calm down.

Withdrawal (difficulty in playing/socialising)

At school children who are deeply grieving may have greater difficulty at playtimes, or at times of group interaction. They will feel themselves to be different and isolated, as they are alone in their grief, particularly if no one else in their class has had a similar experience. They may need extra help to be able to integrate back into the group after a particularly difficult loss, depending on the circumstances and their personality. By withdrawing they are showing that they are not fully making sense of the loss, and that something is happening internally that needs attention. This group can also be prone to bullying, a factor that complicates any response to the situation.

Support ideas

For children who have chosen to withdraw, allowing them safe ways to integrate back into the group is vital. Teachers and other professionals can offer circle time, for example, which involves a safe sharing of feelings and thoughts in a focused way that is facilitated by teaching assistants. Organising certain activities during breaks and lunchtimes can also be useful, so that these children are not left on their own at times when lessons are not taken.

It is also important to help children who withdraw to express their emotions safely, which they are currently not able to do, as well enabling them to see the link between their behaviour and their feelings. Using some of the exercises in Chapter 6: A Toolkit of Activities (such as the Worry Activities 15-18), and sitting with them in a quiet, discreet place to check out how they are doing can be very helpful. Always check that the child wants this extra attention; children who withdraw are hiding away and giving a message that they do not want to be noticed, but when offered attention sensitively they often respond positively. Examples of what to say include:

> *'I have noticed that you stay quiet and on your own at break time and even in the class. Is there any way you would like some extra company?'*

> *'I wonder if being quiet is keeping you from saying what you really need? I know how difficult it has been recently and perhaps what you would like is to sit quietly in a corner and tell me some of what is happening? We can meet when everyone else is out playing if you like, as I know you don't want anyone to see you.'*

> *'You know, when a child has the sort of experiences you have had recently, they usually feel a bit upset, sad or angry. Are any of these what you are feeling, and would you like to talk to someone about this? We could arrange to go somewhere else if here is not a good idea for you.'*

Inability to concentrate

Children who are bereaved often have great difficulty in concentrating on the normal lessons and everyday matters at school or at home. This is very similar to adults, who may respond to grief by becoming vague and forgetful. This is a normal reaction to loss and is one that should gradually fade; school professionals can help by enabling a child to be in a quiet place for some of the day, or having someone to talk to if needed.

Support ideas

Give a child a time-out card (a discreet permission for the child to leave the classroom without having to ask), which will help them to ask for space in order to take their time to recover. As well as using time-out cards, it can be helpful to find a place for the child to go that feels safe and secure, such as a quiet library or reading corner. Offering a child time to talk privately with someone about how they feel can help when a child is unable to concentrate, since this problem indicates the level of emotional confusion the child is experiencing. Examples of what to say include:

> *'I've noticed how hard it is for you to do your work for any length of time since [event that caused loss] happened. I wonder if you need some space away in a quiet room to talk to someone now and then, or just to relax, because children who experience what you have sometimes just find it hard to always do the things they used to do?'*

'Perhaps we can think of ways to help you when you find it hard to concentrate? We can see that you are affected by what has just happened and I know that children feel all sorts of strange feelings and confusions after something like that. I wonder if you want to have some help to find out how you feel?'

Strange behaviours

Sometimes children are so challenged by the experience of their loss that their behaviour becomes more unusual, for example: repetitive behaviour, such as walking round in circles; obsessive behaviour, such as only eating one thing; excessive cleaning; or even needing to talk without stopping. Any of these signs are an indicator of severe distress and will probably need the intervention of a mental health professional to help the child reach a more normal state of grief.

Case study

Jennifer was a 6-year-old who had lost her mother a month earlier to cancer. She had been told what had happened, but had not fully understood the concept of death or that her mummy had been seriously ill. She did not attend her mother's funeral, due to her mother's wishes. She began to become taken with the idea of stars, as she had been told that her mother was now a star. She drew them everywhere, she asked where they were, and finally she asked when her 'mother star' was coming back. She was very, very withdrawn at all other times, only becoming animated when she was talking or asking about stars. She was also not sleeping well. By drawing stars with her, the teacher began to understand her confusion and communicated this to her father and the relatives who were looking after her. They used books to help her understand what death actually meant and how her mummy had died. They then took her to her mother's grave, something they had avoided doing up until then, so that she could begin to make sense of the fact her mother was not coming back.

Conclusions

As can be seen, children show their loss in many ways and it can often be difficult for adults to know whether expressed behaviours and emotions are related to the loss. Some reactions are mild, some are severe and most do not need external help. Often, simply having someone supportive available to talk to, prompt, or offer extra quiet time, can be enough for grieving children. Most children are robust and resilient, particularly if they have had a reasonably secure upbringing prior to the loss. The signs of distress described above and the suggestions for alleviating that distress should therefore prove significant in supporting the vast majority of children suffering from loss, particularly bereaved children.

Chapter 5
How to Help

Where do people go to when they die?
Somewhere down below or in the sky?
'I can't be sure,' said Grandad, 'but it seems
they simply set up homes inside our dreams.'

Jeanne Willis, 'Inside our Dreams', *Toffee Pockets* 2003

Schools occupy a privileged position in the lives of most young children, as children spend much of their lives in and around the school environment. Teachers and assistants often get to know children extremely well, and later in life many adults will describe how one teacher or another was very significant for them when growing up.

With this in mind, it is very useful for schools to know how they can help when children experience loss without, of course, detracting from the main work of education. Whether this is done through talking, providing non-verbal support, monitoring the child's needs, or in other ways (such as keeping in touch with families), school professionals play a role that can be vital in supporting children who have experienced loss.

Other professionals, such as health professionals and social workers, can also use their roles with children to enable greater support at times of loss, depending on the level of contact they have with the child. Parents and carers have the most vital job of all in supporting their own children and, with just a little guidance, they can make a profound difference if the experience of loss is supported in the best possible way.

Indications that a child requires more support

Signs of distress, either overt or concealed, usually mean that a child needs extra attention. These signs may be especially evident at certain times on the child's journey of loss, such as when they are deeply affected by their grief as a result of anniversaries or something else that has triggered memories. Key indicators that a child needs additional support are: 1) behaviour that is out of character for the particular child; 2) extreme behaviour; and 3) behaviour that could be damaging to the child or those around them. The following behaviours may indicate that the child is in need of more support at school or at home:

- Isolation in one form or another (such as not talking much and not playing with others) can be a sign of withdrawal and the need for extra attention.

- Clinging to one teacher or one adult excessively (including at playtimes) is often a sign that a child would like adult support.

- A child who shows a lack of concentration, either in lessons or assembly, and is normally able to concentrate well, is displaying a need for more time to adjust to their loss.

- Distress at times such as Mother's and Father's Day can be a clear sign that the child is remembering their loss and experiencing heightened feelings.

- A child who chooses not to eat at all or only small amounts, or a child who eats excessively, or appears unusually hungry, can often be showing signs of distress that is related to their loss.

- An extreme change of personality in a child, such as from being very quiet to very loud or vice versa, may indicate that the child has some internal responses to their loss that are having a profound effect.

- A child who is continuously asking questions, whether related to their loss or not, may actually have many questions relating to their loss that they have not yet asked.

- A child who looks very sad but insists they are fine, or a child who cannot stop crying for a prolonged periods, can often be showing some need for extra emotional support.

- A very angry child who is always getting into trouble or fighting in the playground, if that child is known to have a loss in their life.

- A child who often arrives at school early or leaves very late is showing by their actions that it is difficult to leave home or difficult to be at home. Sometimes a child who has experienced loss prefers to be at school, perhaps because home is such a difficult and sad place to be, which reminds them of their loss. At other times home is where they would prefer to be, because this is where a child feels safe or wants to remember their loved one.

Guidelines for offering support

- Be aware of the environment if you talk with a child who is bereaved or experiencing loss; they need a safe, discreet place to be able to be honest emotionally. Provide a quiet place, perhaps a room like a library; do not choose to talk in front of the child's friends or just after playtime or just before lunch. At home the place can be a warm, relaxing bedroom, and the time a cosy time after tea.

- Check to make sure that the child wants to talk about their loss, rather than forgetting about it for the moment and running off to play.

- Be aware of the details of the child's loss and experience; school professionals will have to contact carers and parents.

- Be aware that the experience of loss recurs and some loss experiences, such as complicated bereavement, return at times such as anniversaries and life transitions. A file that follows a child as throughout the school and a robust school bereavement policy can help support ongoing feelings of loss. See Chapter 7: Resources, Template for a School Bereavement Policy, for more information.

- Be aware of the friendship groups within the school, since children may gain much support from their friends. Parents and carers can involve friends if, for example, the child appears to become isolated by missing school or other activities. School professionals can offer a friend to be an ally if a child needs time out, for example, and they can help support staff members who are themselves supporting children.

- Be aware of any other support that might be available, particularly if it is clear that a child is struggling in spite of the best efforts of school and colleagues, parents and carers. This support can include other agencies such as counselling services, as well as statutory support such as psychological services.

- Be reflective and responsive in comments, rather than trying to make everything 'all right' again. Most children know that after a loss things will never be the same, so a reflective comment about how they might be feeling or what is happening may give them the confidence that they are supported.

- Give a child choices, so that they can choose for themselves the level of support they want and how to respond to their grief; they need to know there is no right or wrong way to react when they experience loss.

What to say

Children need honest and clear communication when death and loss occurs. This, in turn, gives them permission to talk openly about how they feel, what they need, and to ask any questions they may have. Mention of the obvious (such as the death or the separation) can relieve the tension or the confusion a child may feel about the experience of their loss, and can result in a more open way of coping with their feelings and their life after the loss.

Approach children who have experienced a severe loss with sensitivity: be discreet and find a quiet corner to talk with them, trying not to single them out in front of their friends if they seem uncomfortable. Talking in break time or over lunch is often more appropriate, as your conversation may cause strong feelings to surface and it can be hard for a child to find time to process these emotions during a busy school day.

When a child has experienced bereavement, it is fine to say, for example:

> *'I am sorry to hear your mother/father/sibling/carer/etc. has died.'*

This gives the child permission to speak about it to you later if they wish. Mention of the funeral and asking if they went can also open up conversation about the loss. For example:

> *'I wonder if you were able to say goodbye, either by going to the funeral or in some other way?'*

In this way a child is encouraged to be open about what has happened and to talk about the loss if they have previously not found ways of mentioning it; the acknowledgement of the loss also helps support their grief. You could follow these comments with a question such as:

> *'Is there anyone in school who you could talk to or with whom you would like to sit for five minutes?'*

Such an approach is also a great way of finding out who the child feels they can turn to at times of distress.

It is important to remain open and honest, perhaps checking that a child understands what has happened and whether they would like to know more. If the loss is from a cause such as a separation, children usually like to know exactly what has happened to their loved ones. Make comments that will allow children to ask questions about the situation and enable a supportive, open discussion about their needs, for example:

> *'Your father has had to go abroad for his job. I wonder how you feel about that?'*

> *'We are not going to live together any more as we have decided to separate/divorce. I wonder how you feel about that?'*

> *'I wonder how you are feeling about what has happened?'*

All of these give the child an opening if they need to express how upset or sad or angry they feel. To the child who may be trying desperately not to cry, you could say:

> *'Tell me if you would just like some time alone.'*

What to do

Sometimes school staff find it hard to be proactive when faced with children who are experiencing profound loss. However, just as it is fine to say things more openly about loss, so is it useful to act and prepare for a child's needs. A child who experiences loss needs to feel safe, to have someone to turn to if they wish, not to feel different, and to carry on as normally as possible. They will also need reassurance that the feelings they have are not unusual, that they are not to blame, and that it is normal to feel what they are feeling. There are many ways in which you can ensure that children feel more supported in their loss, even when they are in the depths of despair.

- Help a child to feel safe by allowing them to bring in a toy from home or a picture of the person whom they have lost.

- Give them a time-out card (a discreet permission for the child to leave the classroom without having to ask each time), and find a place for them to sit or be if they need this time away from the class. The use of this card reassures a child who has experienced loss that they are supported by the school. It can reduce the pressure to concentrate or to be happy if they are confused or unhappy. It also gives the child an opportunity to be quiet or time to cry and reflect. On their return to the classroom their concentration will have improved and they will feel happier and more peaceful.

- Find out who they would trust to talk to or sit with if they feel distressed about their loss, and arrange for this person to be available if needed. If a child is unsure who they can trust, you could suggest that it might be a friend or an older child. If you offer the company of this person at certain infrequent times, a child can feel that they have someone to talk to when they feel particularly distressed during the day.

- Offer to keep the child in contact with their parent or carer, as they may become more insecure as a result of the loss and need reassurance that their parent or carer, or sibling, is fine. The method of keeping in contact can be agreed in advance with the family.

- Ask the child how they are doing and whether they need anything. This is such a fundamental question, but it is a useful one because it gives the child the choice of whether to respond or not.

- Check with the family what details they would like other people to know about the situation. This is a valuable way of both keeping in touch with the family and respecting their needs.

- Check with the child what they would like other pupils in their class or school to know. In this way, a child can choose if they would like the whole school to know, or just their class. Occasionally, a child is scared of being seen as different and wishes to pretend a loss has not happened. In this case it is best to explain to the child that some people must know, because the teachers are there to support them. It is also advisable to ask if just one or two of their friends can be told of their loss. Encouraging a child who has experienced loss to be open about this loss can help them to grieve or cope with the loss, whether it is a divorce, separation or bereavement. Other children in the school who have experienced a similar loss can be particularly helpful as support. This can also help reduce the sense of isolation a child nearly always feels at this time.

- Make sure teachers and school support staff know what has happened, so that the child does not have to keep repeating explanations. Some schools like to appoint a key person to liaise with the family, and this is often a good method of communicating with a family in distress. Depending on the wishes of the family, this also allows teachers and school support staff to be aware of a child's potential needs during their loss without having to ask the child directly. See Chapter 7: Resources, for a template of a letter that can be sent home with children.

- Anticipate that the child may need special support at times like Mother's and Father's Day, and special events like birthdays and Christmas. In this way certain difficult dates can be acknowledged for the child, and the experience of anniversaries (during which feelings of loss are always heightened) can be supported.

- Ask the child if they would like to make a Father's Day or Mother's Day card (depending on the person the child has lost). Children continue to feel they have a mother or a father long after that person has died, because they are known to keep their connection to their loved ones alive in this way. Paradoxically, by remembering their parents and what they shared together when the parents are no longer there, a bereaved child will feel more secure and will be enabled to continue developing normally. For more information on this, see Chapter 1: Theories of Bereavement & Loss.

A child experiencing loss is often surprised to hear from adults that the way they are feeling is as a result of their loss. This can in itself be a useful step forward for a child whose feelings are very confused and out of control. It can be helpful to introduce the child to some of the bereavement books for children discussed in Chapter 7: Resources.

How to involve other children

Children who experience loss need to know that they are not isolated, and that they can continue to learn and play normally. For a child who has been bereaved to feel this, they may need extra support to play or to be interactive in the classroom and the playground so that they feel a part of the group. These suggestions should help teachers and school support staff to reintegrate a child who may have been off school for a little while back into their school environment.

Circle time

Offer a circle-time discussion for all children to talk about their feelings. Circle times are now very popular as a part of emotional literacy programmes, and are a way of enabling children to be open about their feelings, to relax together, to build good relationships and to have a time (separate from teaching time) to communicate. Using circle time in this way enables the child who has experienced loss to avoid becoming the centre of attention, whilst still receiving the support they may need from their peer group. Some of the exercises in Chapter 6: A Toolkit of Activities are suitable for circle times. See also resource section at the end for books on circle time.

General assembly

Offer a general assembly on bereavement, divorce and loss. Assemblies bring the whole school together and can be used to offer general education on how families and children experience bereavement, separation and the resultant loss. They can also be used to inform a school, in a safe way, of the loss of someone important to one of the children if the families give permission for this. This, in the same way as a circle-time session, takes the attention away from the individual child who is experiencing loss, whilst still offering that child support.

Assemblies can be quite general, covering aspects of bereavement such as funeral services and forms of burial in different traditions, and can include some introduction to the language and emotions of loss. A simple assembly would include a prayer or the reading of lines that reflect on the way in which some things do not last for ever; the concept of loss could then be introduced, followed by a mention (if appropriate) of the person who has died. See the suggestions in Chapter 7: Resources for guidance on dealing with bereavement in general assemblies.

Small groups

If possible identify at least one or two children who have experienced a similar loss. In this way the child will have access to peer support without having to explain all that they are experiencing. Children who experience loss, particularly from death, often say that knowing someone in a similar situation is a great help to them. It both lessens the sense of isolation they may have, and enables them to see that other children have survived what they are experiencing.

Facilitate a small group so that those with similar types of losses can share experiences. This is not always possible. However, if it is, the group experience is one of the best ways a child can feel supported, learn to live with their loss, share their feelings and feel less isolated. One important factor children often mention when talking about losing someone close to them is that they feel *different*. Being able to attend or be in a group can reduce some of this feeling. If teachers or teaching assistants lack confidence in supporting such a group, a health professional or bereavement expert can sometimes be available to support this and train the teachers. Alternatively, look for bereavement services in the area. See Chapter 7: Resources for the websites of national bereavement services that may be able to help.

Classrooms

During a relevant lesson, introduce a discussion about the children's general experiences of feeling loss, such as the loss of pets, grandparents, moving house, school, or other. This can be a specific lesson on loss or a general lesson on life skills. This general discussion can be a reminder that all children experience loss in some form of another. It not only lessens the isolation of a child during a heightened experience of loss, it also enables and encourages the empathy of other children towards the child.

Buddy systems

Arrange a buddy system throughout the school. A buddy system enables children to support each other openly, with agreed arrangements planned in advance. A child experiencing loss can therefore use this system in the knowledge that it is there for all children, and may be more inclined to ask for support from a 'buddy' if they need it.

Notes on bullying

This is an aspect of loss that requires careful monitoring, because a child who has been bereaved is more susceptible to bullying – and to bullying others. Most schools have a bullying policy and regard this as effective. However, being particularly vigilant on behalf of children who are more vulnerable (such as a bereaved child or one who has just undergone a separation) can be of immense value in reinforcing the policy.

Bullying starts with the recognition that an individual within a group is 'different', or seems separate in some way. Therefore one way to counteract any bullying is to ensure that the child is not isolated, that some wider education on how children experience loss is undertaken, and that the empathetic response of other children is encouraged.

Most bullies are affected by being exposed to their own behaviour. At the early stages of a child's loss you could emphasise to the class and to friends that the child will need their friends more than usual, and that if anyone sees something unfriendly happening they should tell a teacher. It is sometimes hard to find out exactly what happens when bullies are actually bullying others. Having a meeting between bully and the bullied can be effective sometimes, as long as the child bullying actually apologises and learns that they should not have done so.

Sometimes vigilance is simply the best way to stop bullying, and it may be enough to give children the confidence to report bullying to a teacher – or to a friend who will then tell a teacher for them. Bullies thrive on secrecy and by their very nature are cowards, so it is very important that if bullying begins with a child who is more sensitive due to their loss, the school treats the bullying as a whole school incident rather than keeping it between the child and the bully. An assembly on bullying and how wrong it is may be the best response. This not only keeps the target away from the child being bullied, it also allows other children to consider their experience of bullying and opens the whole topic.

What not *to say*

In the same way as it is possible to give guidelines covering helpful things to say to children suffering loss, there are also guidelines as to what is definitely *not* helpful. A child may become confused about, for example, the nature of death, their role in it, or what has happened to their loved one. They may feel isolated or rejected and believe they should not have the feelings they do have. Any actions or comments that lead to these outcomes could be said to be unhelpful for a child experiencing loss. Do not say, for example:

'You'll be alright soon, just forget it.'

This is simply a denial of the feelings they are experiencing, and can lead to a child pretending they are feeling happy when in fact they are not. It also denies the fact that grief and loss feelings do not disappear overnight but come and go, often over a long period of time.

'They have gone to sleep for ever.' (Rather than 'they are dead'.)

Telling a child their loved one has gone to sleep forever can lead them to become very afraid of sleep and to have nightmares, or alternatively they may hope that by sleeping themselves they will meet their loved one again. It can be very confusing, particularly for young children, to have an association between death and sleep, as they may also become very afraid that someone else sleeping will die.

'It's silly to have worries about your mum/dad/sister/brother.'

A child who is feeling loss and grief will nearly always have some worries, and it is far better to attempt to discover what these worries are than to undermine that anxiety.

'It's not a good idea to cry, as you will just upset yourself.'

In saying this, a child is being told that it is not acceptable to have the feelings of sadness and upset associated with loss. However, this can then lead to a child feeling much more confused and believing that these feelings are wrong or bad in some way. Most children will cry for a short time and then be able to recover themselves, returning to playing or attending lessons.

'Don't make such a fuss of it; others have a lot worse time than you.'

By comparing a grieving child to other children, this sort of comment can create a similar reaction to the previous one, leading to a belief that the feelings they have are wrong or bad in some way. As the grieving child's need will be to feel that they are not the only one who has experienced loss, the child will be confused to be compared to others in a detrimental way, as opposed to a positive, supportive way.

'Heaven doesn't really exist, you know.'

Even children whose upbringing does not include a religion or faith can have thoughts about heaven when someone dies. It is usually better to try and discover what a child might believe happens in heaven than to deny it exists. By denying that heaven exists, a child may have lost a very important source of comfort related to where their loved one has gone. Having a concrete idea of where their relative is, whether this is heaven or elsewhere, can be very important as a child adjusts to their loss.

> *'You must be the man of the house now.'*

If this comment is made to quite young children, sometimes when a father has left or died, it can be a huge burden on a child, since they will normally take it quite seriously. The main danger is that they will try to take on adult concerns and responsibilities too soon.

> *'They are not coming back and that is that; now you must get on with things.'*

All people who are bereaved, both children and adults, go through a stage when they believe their loved one is coming back or wonder if they are coming back. If a child who is experiencing loss is told bluntly that the deceased is not coming back, this can block this stage of grief and lead to more confusion at a time when they have not yet adjusted to their loss. It is better to ask if they know what death means and if they understand that it is permanent, before explaining that they might find it hard at first to believe this.

> *'[Name of person] is always watching over you so you have to be good.'*

This is a very typical comment made by adults who believe it is helpful. However, when a child who has experienced loss is told this, they will literally believe they are being watched over. This can lead to a feeling of pressure to be good, to perform well and to attempt to be on their best behaviour all the time. This can cause a lot of confusion for a typical child who needs to be able to play and release feelings, but might not want to for fear of upsetting their loved one.

What not to do

- Do not make a child the centre of attention when they do not want to be, or single them out in front of others and pointedly ask them how they are. A child who is experiencing loss may or may not wish for attention, since this depends on their personality, the nature of the loss and how confident they are that school can meet their needs. It is far better to first check with the child if they would like this attention given to them.

- Do not ignore the child when they are upset or having a difficult day. Again, this will depend on the personality of the child, as some children who are shy or quiet, may prefer to be upset quietly, whereas others will want to be comforted and reassured that it is normal to have the feelings they are experiencing as a result of their loss. It is important, however, for teachers and school assistants to check with the child whether they prefer to be alone or not.

- Do not refuse to let them make a Father's Day or Mother's Day card if their father or mother has died. When a child is bereaved of a father or mother, they will continue to feel connected to them internally and emotionally, and will nearly always want to make a card on their special days. This helps the child in their grieving process and in the adjustment as they get older. This is because memories (particularly good memories) remain a part of a child's internal self and enable the child to grow through various stages of development. See Chapter 1: Theories of Bereavement & Loss for further information about this.

- Do not push them to work harder if they are having difficulty concentrating. One of the symptoms of bereavement is a difficulty in concentrating, and this is true for both adults and children. A child who has experienced loss, therefore, will typically have more difficulty concentrating on lessons, although some children focus more on school to forget their loss. If a child is struggling after a loss, it is more appropriate to give them some extra time or extra support so that they can do the work at their own pace.

- Do not refuse to let them leave the classroom if they are upset, sad or angry due to the loss. As mentioned earlier, it is normally helpful for a child to be able to leave the classroom and find a safe place or person if they wish this. Being upset or experiencing another emotion within a classroom setting can be very distressing for a child who has experienced loss, and they are often likely to wish for more privacy at this time.

- Do not forget to speak to the child's carer or family. It is often best if the school makes contact with a family when a loss has occurred, for some of the reasons mentioned earlier. In particular, families can find it difficult to approach teachers or to know what to say, and if the school offers support without being asked this enables a family to choose what to say. A simple query about how the family are managing and whether or not they would like the children in the child's class to know about the loss is often enough to allow them to choose whether they wish to say more or not.

- Do not ignore questions about death because you do not know what to say. A teacher or school assistant can sometimes find it difficult to speak of death and related feelings, particularly when difficult questions are asked, such as 'What does it feel like when you are dead?', and 'Where has my [relative] gone?' However, with more confidence, most professionals can help children openly speak of their experiences of loss and how they feel. It is fine to say that you do not know what happens when a person dies, but that you know sometimes people get very upset. What children need most of all, however, is to understand that the loved one is not coming back, can no longer breathe, be in pain, speak, walk, talk or do anything we do. This can then enable a child who has experienced loss to also be able to speak of these things.

To end on a positive note: if the positive and honest comments in the 'What to say' section are repeated frequently enough, both children and adults will gain confidence in acknowledging their loss, the pain of knowing the loved is not coming back, and the fact that death is part of life and has entered the life of the bereaved child too soon.

How to remain in touch with the family

🖐 Arrange for a special letter to be sent home to offer support, if needed, immediately after a death. See Chapter 7: Resources for a template of a suitable letter. Families can be confused both about when it is appropriate to send a child back to school, and what form of support is available. By sending a letter detailing some of the available support, along with offers of condolence, a family can approach the school without fear of rejection and will feel more confident about discussing the child's needs with school staff.

🖐 Be proactive in asking family members how they are doing and how they think their child is managing the loss. In this way the family is being supported alongside the child, and you are helping them to communicate better. Families and carers who have experienced a loss are often numb, confused and unsure what to tell schools, and this gives them an open invitation to have conversations that can be helpful for the school and themselves in supporting the responses to their loss.

🖐 Offer to send work home from school if the child needs to take time off. Parents and carers can be very reluctant for children to take this time off. However, this may be just what the child needs if they are very distressed and simply cannot concentrate on anything or engage with the normal daily activities of school. A few days off from school can be supportive to both child and family as they adjust to life with their loss, and because the offer to send work home has been made families will feel less guilty that they are taking their child away from important education activities.

🖐 Arrange for a card signed by the whole class to be sent if the child has not returned to school immediately after the loss. This not only prepares the child for active support when they return, but also offers the child a link into their friends and support network, so that they can choose who they turn to on return. This card should only be sent, however, if a family is clear that they wish the class to know of their loss.

🖐 Be available at drop-off and pick-up times in particular, as these are times of heightened anxiety for children following a loss, and can be the most difficult transitions between home and school. A child will often be afraid that something else will happen at home or with their family immediately after a loss, from whatever cause. This will cause anxieties which need to be allayed, and having a teacher present alongside the family member to support their arrival and departure can bring comfort that there are adults present both at home and at school helping them to feel safe again.

🖐 Ask if the family would like a special meeting to discuss anything they may be worried about; don't assume that families will ask for this themselves, as they often are reluctant to ask for special favours or call attention to their situation at a vulnerable time.

🖐 If families are reluctant to talk to the school professionals, for whatever reason, it is sometimes useful to adopt the casual phone call approach in order to find out what is happening and if they feel their child is doing reasonably well. This can be followed by a letter if the school has concerns about how a child is managing. Most parents and carers do care, but may sometimes be caught up in their own concerns and grief, whatever the cause of their loss. A regular phone call, a follow-up letter and a casual meeting at the beginning or end of day can be far better than calling a family in for an official meeting, unless there are serious concerns.

When to call in other professionals

There is no hard and fast rule as to when it is best to look for someone extra such as a counsellor or play therapist to support young people in grief and loss. The clearest indication that this might be necessary is normally that the child is clearly not functioning well, either in the classroom, elsewhere, or at home, and that this has been continuing for some time.

Indications that professional help is needed can include showing severe signs of depression, anger or withdrawal, an inability to speak to people, to eat, or to play with others. Some or all of the examples of physical and emotional reactions in Chapter 4: The Different Ways Children Express Loss & How to Support Them are useful indicators.

The importance of the length of time a behaviour is exhibited depends on the nature of what the child is showing; for example, if they are completely refusing to eat this poses a risk to their well-being and cannot be continued for long. However, if the child has been showing extreme anger for a week, this is not very long unless they are severely hurting themselves or others.

Case study

Kayleigh was a shy 5-year-old girl who had not long joined the school. She experienced the death of a much-loved grandmother, and clearly did not fully understand where she had gone. She began to ask all the teachers if they knew where people went when they died and if they came back. She also began to upset the other children with these questions.

The teachers arranged to have a special assembly for all the younger children on death and dying, with the permission of the parents. In this assembly they gave information on the physical reactions to death, talked briefly about funerals and different belief systems in a very simple way, and showed some examples in nature for all the children to touch, such as autumn leaves, and a dying flower.

They also offered a meeting with Kayleigh's mum to ask what she had been told about her grandmother, so that they could support this. Kayleigh had been regarded as too young to go to the funeral and her parents had thought she was fine as she had shown no interest when told her gran had died. As a result of this meeting, her mum sat and talked with her about where her grandmother was and that it was normal to be sad about this, and school supported this with some books and comments that could be used if she continued to ask questions.

The class followed up the assembly with a circle time on loss, in which they discussed things like pets that have died and the passing seasons, and one child opened up to the experience of his own loss due to separation. The children were more able to support each other as a result of this loss, and Kayleigh began to understand that her grandmother was not coming back, becoming appropriately sad at times.

Case study

Daniel was a boy of 8 years old who had experienced a few changes due to his dad being in the army. His family had lived abroad for some time, and he had attended at least two other schools. He had been in his current school for the past year and was beginning to make good friends, but he had a tendency to call attention to himself.

He arrived one day at school and began to be very angry. He had a fight in the playground and needed to be calmed down. At first he was simply told off. However, one of the teachers took him to one side and asked him what was going on. He told her it was because his dad had gone away again, and he did not know where, or for how long. The teacher had recently attended a course on bereavement and loss, and so she was aware that his reaction was due to his experience of having to say goodbye again to his dad without knowing if he was coming back. She was able to use some reflective comments to assure him that she would not just dismiss what he said and asked if she could talk to his mum about this. He agreed.

The class teacher was able to make contact with his mum and to talk on the phone about what was happening at home. His mum was also distressed, because they had apparently not expected his dad to be called away on active service so soon. She had thought Daniel was fine. They talked through what might be helpful for Daniel and ways in which the school could support her. As a result of this conversation Daniel was told more about his dad's departure, including where his dad was going to be and how they could keep in touch by email, phone and computer linking. His mum also began to seek out the teacher to talk if she had been having a bad day herself, and the school was able to link her to other mothers in a similar situation. Daniel's anger calmed down once he was told more, and he learnt to ask for help when he felt himself losing control. School identified one key person who would be available for him if he was particularly worried, and he began to make new friends again.

Chapter 6
A Toolkit of Activities

In this chapter you will find photocopiable resources and suggestions that can be used with individual children or groups, depending on the activity. These practical resources are divided into the following sections:

1 Exercises for enabling feelings
2 Exercises for working with specific feelings
3 Exercises for telling the story of loss
4 Exercises for treasuring memories
5 Questions

The activities are all tried and tested ways of supporting children's feelings and their adjustment to loss. They can empower children to make good memories from difficult ones, to recognise the point at which they need to ask adults for more help, and may also be used to introduce aspects of loss to a group or class of children in a safe, manageable way. They are easy to use, and most adults will be able to support children in the activities.

When undertaking activities related to bereavement and loss, it is important to prepare your sessions carefully and to manage your activities so that the children involved gain maximum benefit according to their own needs.

Preparation

Prepare yourself well for each exercise. Make sure you know what is needed and what responses you may get. This includes preparing for practical needs, such as paper and crayons, as well as emotional preparation.

Emotional preparation

Check that you are emotionally ready for questions and comments about such a highly charged subject. This subject affects adults as much as children, and if any of the adults leading the exercises have had their own bereavement, for example, they should acknowledge that the children's responses and questions might upset them by reminding them of their own loss. It is usually best if people who are recently bereaved do not facilitate these exercises, although if children know that one of their teachers has experienced their own bereavement it can actually reassure them.

It is fine for children to know that adults have been upset in the past by loss, but it is usually better not to show them the strongest emotions in a classroom. It is also not surprising to know that children are very quick to pick up on the feelings adults have about this topic and will unconsciously be affected by them, even if they are not aware of this. The more you can be clear and honest about how you feel, the more relaxed the children will feel in using these exercises to access their own feelings and responses. If they sense that you are fearful of responses that may trigger your own emotions, they may be too guarded in their interaction to benefit fully from the exercises.

The same thing applies to parents, carers and other professionals who may use these activities. Make sure that you are emotionally, as well as practically, prepared. This is particularly important if you are a carer, foster carer or parent who has emotional involvement with both the child and the loss. Be honest with yourself in acknowledging that your own feelings will probably be aroused by this topic, and be honest with your children also. If you know that the loss or bereavements you have had are recent and have affected you deeply, you may be upset in front of the children. Sometimes it can be helpful to do some of these exercises on your own to check your responses. In this way you can decide in advance if you are comfortable sharing your own feelings with children. It is sometimes very appropriate for children to see adults upset, as this helps them understand that strong feelings are acceptable when a loss has happened. It is, however, usually more appropriate to find the time to share these feelings in advance of starting the exercises. Only you will know if your sensitivity to this subject means it is hard for you to support your child through the exercises.

If you find that you are becoming upset in the course of an activity, do not stop the activity, but perhaps tell your child:

> '*I may get upset when you do this, but that is OK as we have all been affected by this loss. Don't let that stop you doing what you need.*'

Alternatively, you can hold onto your feelings until you are somewhere you can let them out safely on your own. Adults who care for children who have experienced a loss or bereavement usually need their own support networks, whether it be friends, family or more professional support such as counselling. In finding your own network of support, your children will be reassured that they can access the support you are offering them without worrying about your feelings and responses.

Practical preparation

Prepare the room, tables and resources for the activities in advance. Remember to keep the environment safe and relaxed, as issues relating to loss can be very challenging for children with direct experience of it.

Time and place

You could choose a quiet corner that is normally the reading area, or a separate room where the children can remain undisturbed and quiet. Think about the time of day you will do these activities. It is better to do them when you will have a period of time before the children have to rush off to another activity, or even lunch. Ensure that you have planned enough time for questions, upset feelings, and for discussion and reflection time as a group, as well as individually. Also ensure that you do not have a pressing engagement immediately after in case children need more time or some time out after an exercise.

Seating arrangements

Although you should not be afraid to change the size of the groups and the seating arrangements depending on the activity, you could consider the following when planning each activity:

- How many children will sit at a table;

- How many children can undertake an activity at any one time;

- Who in the class or group has experienced recent bereavement or loss and may need to be close to other children less affected by loss; and

- Who has difficulty in group situations.

Creating a relaxing environment

The more safe a child feels in your environment, the better they will be able to use the exercises and the more helpful this will be for them. A child's feelings of safety will be increased in a room that is pleasant and relaxing; you can aid relaxation by allowing children to take off their shoes and by having everyone sit on cushions on the carpet for at least some part of the session.

Music can be used to create a relaxed and informative atmosphere, though the choice of music will be significant. Classical music and calming music would obviously be more beneficial than loud rock music, and composers such as Mozart and Bach have been shown to enhance learning as well as relaxation in a classroom. However, as some of these exercises deal with difficult feelings, the music may not always reflect the feelings the children are experiencing, in which case the music can be turned off after the first parts of the exercise are done.

Ensure that the children doing the exercises trust the adults leading them, and let them know that the normal rules of discipline (such as not talking) do not apply. Ensure that all the children know there is no right or wrong in these exercises, and that they can ask questions at any point without getting into trouble. Even if you do not know all their personal histories, you will probably know more than you realise about their needs and their personalities.

Getting the most from your activities

Activities for individual children

The exercises may be undertaken by children working in a group, but there may be children who would benefit from one-to-one time with a teaching assistant or other professional. This is especially useful for children who have had a recent bereavement or loss, or who are asking lots of questions. If you plan to offer special activities to an individual child within a group, remember to make sure that the child is not made to feel too different, perhaps discreetly asking them whether they would like to join another assistant in a separate part of the room or school while the other children do another activity. One of the main issues that often affects bereaved children or those experiencing a loss is a sense of being different from other children, so a way of handling these activities that does not highlight this 'separateness' is important. Do not, therefore, ask these things in front of other children. It can be better to give each child in a group different exercises (perhaps repeating the same exercise several times across the group), rather than singling out one or two children for special treatment.

Introducing an activity appropriately

An activity may, for example, be part of a wider topic of loss, or it may be a separate exercise on feelings or relationships. Link it to an issue or theme that is appropriate to the children in the group, and then remind them that if at any point they become upset or need help, they can ask someone for help. If it is a 'feelings' exercise, remind them that it is an exercise to help them understand their feelings and reassure them that they can ask for help if the feeling becomes too big. This may be particularly important for anger, for example, in which the feeling could get out of control without extra safety and support. Given that strong feelings in the classroom (for example) are not always acceptable, it helps to set out some clear boundaries. You might suggest that children tell a friend or teacher before they get upset, and that they put their hands up to ask questions or if they need help. But make it clear that you are there to help and support, not to discipline. The safer a child feels, the more effective these exercises can be. The aim is to make the exercises safe enough to be useful, even in the classroom.

Use of circle time for activities

Many of these activities can be introduced and followed up in circle-time type activities. During circle times, children are encouraged to explore their own feelings, their sense of relationships to each other and develop some emotional literacy skills (see for example Roffey 2006). Circle times are normally a specific, set-aside time for the children to meet in a group with a teacher or teaching assistant to explore these topics. Aspects of loss and the feelings associated with them are therefore very appropriate for circle times. Children can be encouraged to share as little or as much as they need of the exercises and will develop an empathetic sense of how to support each other alongside asking for help. Activities particularly suited for circle times include the Dice Activities 1 and 3, the Feelings Faces Activity 3 and the Worry Activities (15–18).

If using the activities in circle time, introduce the topic clearly and note the guidance on preparation. Schools who regularly offer circle time can integrate this topic into their schedule easily, ensuring that the children learn to communicate how they feel concerning loss as the topic develops. Schools who have not offered circle time activities before can be guided by researching the books available (see References) for support ideas.

Repeating activities regularly

Decide whether these exercises could be used in a weekly format, such as at circle time or another session. This helps to 'normalise' the otherwise difficult experience of loss for a child, since it will become normal to have such explorations on a regular basis within the classroom setting. You could then introduce the weekly exercise on loss to examine, as a class, how we all manage. The children who usually never say anything are then more likely to use this time to tell their story, which can only be beneficial.

Your own ability to listen and learn

Finally: listen! Children who have been bereaved or have gone through major loss usually need to tell their story, or their feelings, or both. Listening empathetically can make a huge difference to their ability to manage and cope. Even if you cannot listen immediately, try to say something such as:

> *'I am sorry, I cannot listen now, but come back to me later at break/in 10 minutes, as I know how important it is to you.'*

By listening with attention and care, you are giving the message to children who are struggling to make sense of their loss or bereavement that their feelings are important, and that you will try to be there to support them – and that they are not alone.

Enabling Feelings

Activity 1

Making the Feelings Dice

Children are encouraged to make a large dice; each of the six sides represents a feeling that is connected with loss.

👐 This exercise is useful for children who have little emotional literacy. Since dice are usually associated with games, children can begin to make sense of their feelings in a safe and playful way.

👐 Use the exercise to introduce the topic of loss, or to follow on from other exercises identifying feelings that children have when someone experiences loss of any kind. Although this is a loss exercise, it can, of course, be related to other emotional literacy classes that include the exploration of feelings and their identification.

Materials

👐 A Feelings Dice template (p.89), one for each child, cut out in advance of the activity. The original template provided here is A4, but it is advisable to enlarge it by photocopying onto A3 card so that the finished dice will be bigger. Teachers should decide on an appropriate size for each class and age group.

👐 Colouring pens or pencils

👐 Glue

Introducing the activity

👐 Talk about some of the feelings that children can have when they experience loss, including bereavement or upset of any sort.

👐 Explain the Feelings Dice and discuss five of the six feelings for the six sides of the dice: sadness, happiness, anger, fear, confusion.

👐 Ask them for examples, as a class, of what may cause these feelings.

Page 1 of 2

How to make the dice

1   After the discussion about five main feelings, ask the children to draw something that expresses one of these feelings on each of five sides of their own Feelings Dice. Remind them of the examples they suggested before or mention some yourself, such as 'sad' for a pet that died, or 'angry' for when grandma moved out.

2   Suggest they could use a colour to describe the feeling if they do not want to draw an actual event. Alternatively, they can draw feelings faces (see Activity 3: Feeling Faces & Scenarios). It is important to tell them that there is no right or wrong way to draw the feelings.

3   Ask them to think up their own feeling for the sixth side. Tell them this can be anything (a worry or another feeling) and that if they cannot think of a sad feeling, they can draw another happy feeling.

4   After they have drawn on all six sides of the dice, the children can glue their dice together using the flaps. Remember that children may need help during the drawing exercise or in gluing the dice together at the end.

Monitor the children's needs

Remind the children to not let anyone else tell them what to do, as it is important they begin to recognise their own feelings, not someone else's. This can be particularly important for the quiet, less confident child who may be nervous of doing this exercise in front of others. Take particular note of any children who may have had a recent loss. It may be important to choose how your groups of children are arranged, so that a quiet or recently bereaved child is in a group with a friend or someone who has less experience of loss.

Follow-on ideas

The dice is used again in Activity 2. The children can take their own dice home with them or leave it at school. They do not have to put their name on it, as some of the children may want it to be anonymous when they have finished.

Feelings Dice Template

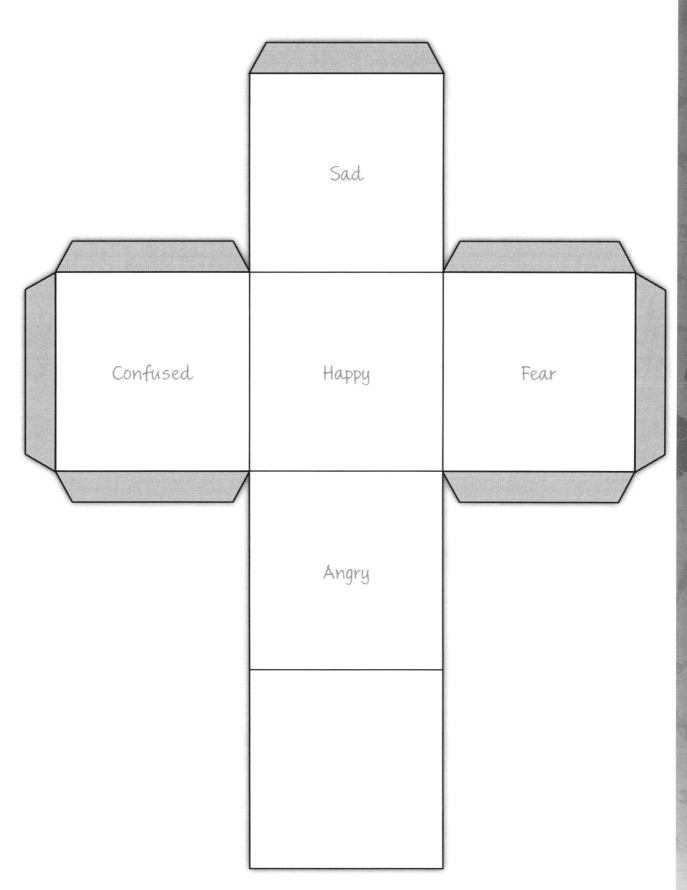

Enabling Feelings Activity 2 Feelings Dice Activities

The children continue to use the Feeling Dice in games and activities that enable them to:

 Talk about their feelings and their losses more openly and safely;

 Share these feelings with an adult if they need to;

 Normalise the experience of loss (almost every child will have had a form of loss even at a young age, although it may be something simple such as seeing an animal dead on the road or a leaf turn brown);

 Understand friends who have experienced serious loss, so that they can support them and empathise with them.

Materials

 A Feelings Dice for each child

Introducing the games

Some suggestions are given below for activities using the Feelings Dice and teachers and carers will be able to make up their own activities as well. Introduce the activities as fun games that might be difficult at times. It is very important to remind children who have experienced loss (particularly difficult loss) that having fun and being happy while they are playing games is acceptable. They do not have to be sad all the time.

Feelings Dice Activities

1   Tell the children that they can keep their dice on their desks or in their trays to use when they want. When they are ready, they can place the dice on their desk so that the feeling they are experiencing at that moment is on the top. Tell them that if the feeling is particularly big and they want to talk about it, they can put their hand up and ask the

Page 1 of 3

teacher to come over and see the dice. This is a very simple way for a bereaved child to begin to express how they are feeling safely.

2   This activity helps children to empathise with each other concerning loss. Place the children in small groups. Tell them that during this exercise they can begin to share what they have drawn on their dice with other children if they want. Ask each child to show the others in their group the side of their own dice that they are most proud of, and to tell the story of why they drew it. Remind the children to take turns and to listen carefully. Teachers may need to facilitate this session by giving quiet children the chance to speak as much as the less quiet ones. Then each group chooses a member of their group to go to the front of the class to tell one of the stories about feelings. If necessary help the groups to decide which story it will be and why; your assistance could be important at this point, because some children (particularly those who have been recently bereaved) will not want to do this, while others will enjoy it. Enabling the quieter children to find the courage to speak could be of benefit to them.

3   The children are offered the chance to display their dice on a table that can be called the 'feelings' table (or the 'loss' table, the 'games' table, the table for 'difficult experiences', and so on). The teacher's role is to keep the displayed dice safe, and to choose those children who are happy to share their dice, while recognising those who would prefer to keep them private. No child should have to share anything during the activity if they do not want to, as some of the feelings may be very private or very strong, and a classroom is not always the best place to feel safe enough to show them openly.

4   During a drama or English lesson, ask the children to make up a story connected to one of the feelings (and the loss that caused it) on their dice. Give them three different characters for a story: the person/animal who died, the person left behind and the person who supports them all. In a drama class you can ask the children to act out an imaginary experience of having that particular feeling. In an English class you can ask the children to make up a story with the three characters that makes use of the feeling they have chosen. Clearly, this sort of lesson must be well planned and prepared for, but can prove a very creative and enjoyable way of understanding feelings related to loss.

5   Hang the dice up in the room in a particular corner, so that they are on display. Use the display to refer to feelings and loss if you are having a lesson connected to loss, or if a child is struggling with their feelings of loss. The child who is struggling could then go and choose a dice to show how they are feeling at that particular time.

6 Use the dice to introduce the Activities for Working with Specific Feelings (Activities 4–24). Ask the children to think back to when they made the dice, and remind them that all the feelings they drew are feelings that people experience when someone dies or moves away.

7 Arrange the children in a circle, using just one dice. One child starts the game and throws the dice to another child within the group; the second child then chooses one side of the dice and tells the rest of the group one thing that may cause this feeling and one thing that can help with this feeling. Then they throw it to the next child, and so on. This gives the children a fun way of talking about feelings and some ways of finding resolution for difficult feelings without becoming stuck in this feeling. Teachers and facilitators can intervene if at any point they either see a child become distressed or if the activity is failing to work properly. An adult in the group could also support the process by modelling their own experience of a feeling and their own way of helping it.

8 Play the Feelings Dice board game, using the following rules:

- Use the template for the board game found on page 93.
- Each child chooses a coloured counter and uses their own dice.
- Everyone in turn places their coloured counter on Start and throws their dice.
- When the dice is thrown, one feeling will be on the top. Each feeling has a different score: (sad=1; happy=2; angry=3; worried=4; frightened=5; and the sixth feeling (chosen by the child when the dice was made)=6.
- The coloured counter is moved the number of places on the board that the child has scored with their dice.
- The children can potentially 'slide' or 'climb' to a higher position on the board if they land on a square with a snake or a ladder.
- Whoever gets to Finish first is the winner.

Feelings Dice Board Game

START

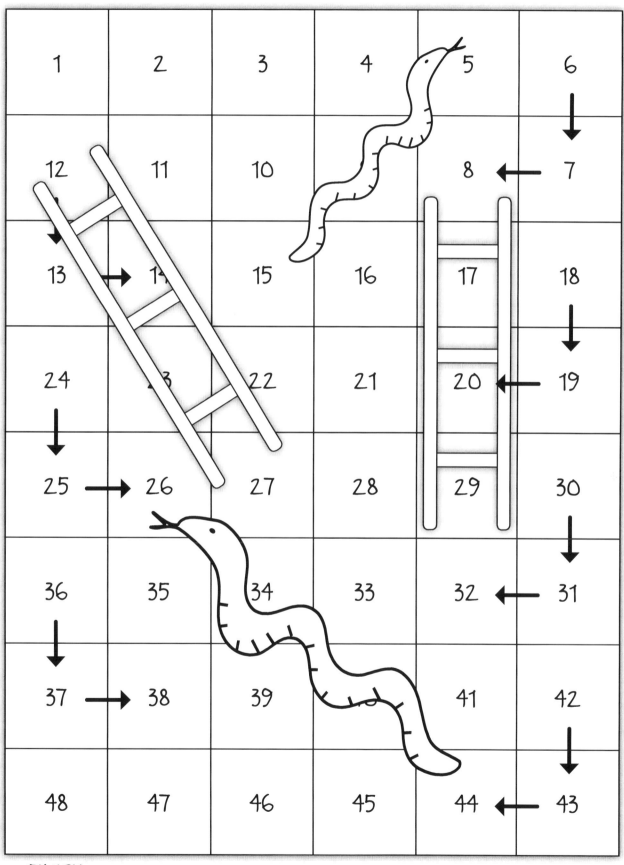

FINISH

Enabling Feelings

Activity 3

Feelings Faces & Scenarios

These activities help reinforce a child's psychological resilience by enabling children to:

- Recognise and express their feelings;

- Gain support for their feelings; and

- Recognise and empathise with the feelings of others.

Materials

- Feelings Faces Worksheet (p.96) several for each child/group

- Empty Feelings Faces Worksheet (p.97) several for each child/group

- Scenarios Worksheet (p.98)

- Coloured pencils or crayons

Activities

1 Give each child/group a sheet of Feelings Faces, then read out a scenario from the Scenarios Worksheet. Ask the children to discuss how they might feel, and then use a Feelings Faces Worksheet to circle or colour the face they think describes the feelings. Remember to prepare the individuals or groups well: discuss the feelings most associated with loss, watch for any particularly vulnerable children, and allow them to choose whether or not they think the exercise is appropriate to join in with.

2 Individual children can use the Feelings Faces to indicate how they feel and any particular needs they have. Give them a Worksheet and ask them to circle the faces most appropriate for how they feel now. Alternatively, ask the children if they have ever felt something similar in their own lives. This can generate a discussion that can lead to a new lesson, if needed. Make sure that the children know they can ask for help if talking about their feelings in this way leads to distress or the need to talk.

Page 1 of 2

3 Use the Empty Feelings Faces Worksheets and ask each child to fill it in with a feeling they have felt in connection to a loss. This can be used in relation to either a class discussion on bereavement or loss, or when a child within the class has experienced a significant loss. It can enable the class both to support their classmate or friend, and also to help other children who have experienced lesser losses.

4 Distribute the Feelings Faces Worksheets with feelings labelled to each group of children. Ask each child or group to select what they think are the two most important feelings relating to loss. This is best done after a class lesson, discussion, or school assembly on the subject of loss. Then ask each group to make up a short story involving each of the feelings they have selected. After they have done this, each group can share their story and the other children can ask questions if necessary. This activity adapts well to a variety of needs, situations and desired results.

5 Ask the children to each choose one Feelings Face. It can be one they have felt a lot, or one they have never felt, or even one they would like to explore. Follow this up by asking each child how they would show that feeling to other children. For example, anger would be by shouting or stamping, sadness would be by sitting and looking lost or not speaking to others. Use prompts to help them decide how they will show these feelings. This exercise both normalises the feelings associated with loss, and educates the children in empathising and supporting each other in preparation for the losses some of them will experience.

Feelings Faces

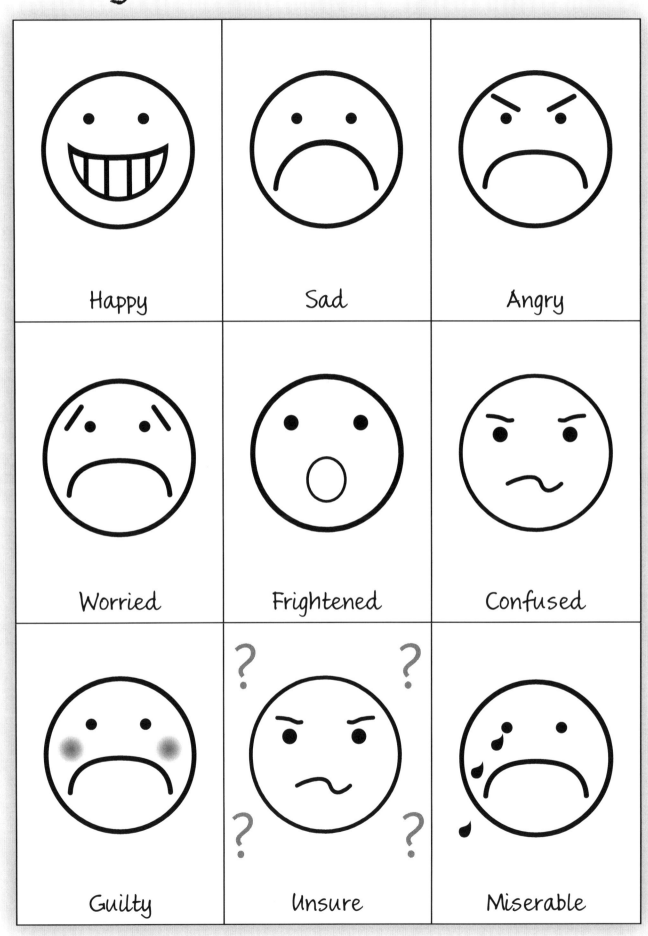

Happy	Sad	Angry
Worried	Frightened	Confused
Guilty	Unsure	Miserable

Empty Feelings Faces

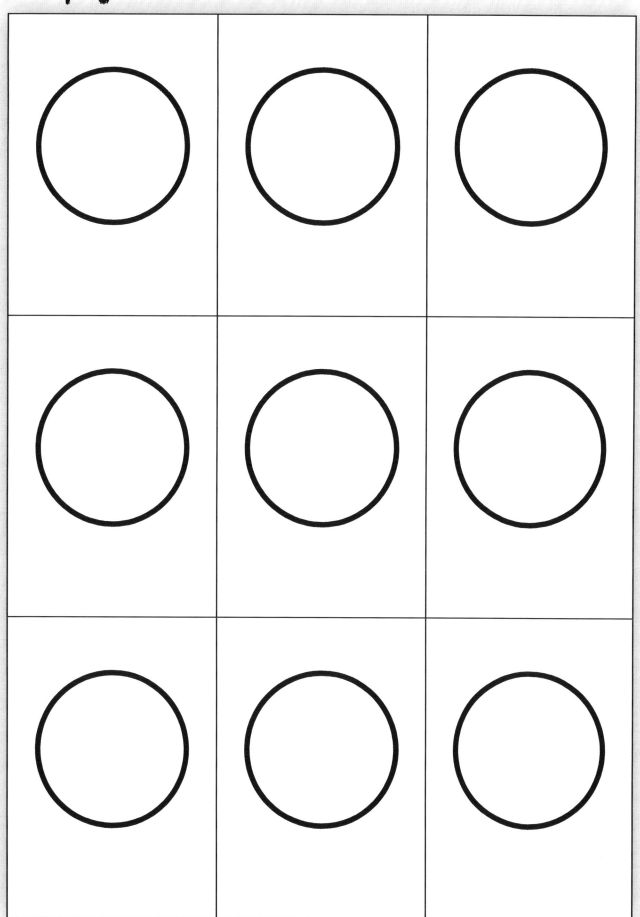

Scenarios Worksheet

1   Your friend has recently been upset, as his mum and dad are arguing a lot. They finally tell him that they are thinking of breaking up and hope he will not be too unhappy.

2   Your mother tells you that she is ill. You are not sure if she is just simply ill or if it is something much worse. You are not sure whether to ask her or your dad.

3   A friend in your class misses school for three days. When she comes back, the class teacher tells you all that her dad has died.

4   Your older sister comes down from breakfast with red eyes. You later learn that she has broken up with her boyfriend.

5   You arrive home from school and your mum sits you down and tells you your pet cat has just died from an illness.

6   You have an argument with your dad in the morning. When you come back from school, you learn that your dad has left home and gone to live somewhere else. Your mum will not tell you any more.

7   You attend a school assembly. At this assembly there is a minute's silence because a child from your school has died from cancer. You later realise that this child was in your class.

8   One of your friends tells you his dad has had to go away. His mum told him this morning, but didn't give him any details. Your friend thinks his dad has gone to prison, as he was in trouble with the police a few months ago, but no one is telling your friend anything.

9   You go out at the weekend and have a great time; but when you get home your mum comes running out of the house telling you there has been an accident and someone is really badly hurt in hospital.

Activities for Specific Feelings
Activities 4-9: Anger

Guidance notes

Anger is a normal and healthy feeling associated with grief and loss. Children who experience loss and grief often feel angry but do not know how to express this or know that in some way it is not usually acceptable. However anger is a normal feeling; for children, the aim is for them to be able to express it safely and not with destruction or against anyone else. Anger can also be associated with getting into trouble, fighting or being aggressive, whereas it is actually a healthy and normal reaction to loss. The distinction that is important to be made for children feeling angry, is that the feeling is acceptable, but destructive behaviour resulting from anger or directed at other people or things is not acceptable.

This is sometimes the first time that children have heard this message. Children who are normally not angry at all can be particularly frightened by the feelings that emerge from their experience of loss. Anger can also be a difficult emotion for both professionals and parents to acknowledge in their children. However, allowing a child to express their anger safely, within the confines of safe exercises can help them to acknowledge and release this feeling and enable healthy grief from loss.

Guidance for professionals

Clearly schools do not normally allow anger to be expressed in the classroom. Therefore, it will be important to emphasise to the child in school that:

- Anger is a normal feeling associated with loss;

- The rules of behaviour of the classroom still apply;

- That doing exercises related to anger can be very helpful for someone who feels it, and is far better than taking anger out on other people or things. This may be the first time that some children will have heard this message.

Prepare the environment and the children by establishing the safety in a classroom or other environment that allows for safe expression of feelings. Talk about what feelings exist, place the children in appropriate groups, the most vulnerable close to friends or a teaching assistant. In addition, decide if the exercises are best used in groups or with individuals.

Page 1 of 2

Always remind children that they can ask a teacher for help at any time.

It may be particularly important with children who have already been noted as showing some signs of out-of-control anger, to monitor their reaction and support them in not becoming out of control.

Supporting them can include telling them it is OK to be angry but not to be destructive, finding a quiet place for them to calm down, checking out how they feel during the exercise, giving them a one-to-one adult time in a separate room, and empathising with their feelings. Sometimes children may need to simply tell their story of loss and be listened to.

Feeling angry safely is one of the most therapeutic ways to allow and manage feelings of loss.

Guidance for parents and carers

- Remember to reassure your children that they will not get into trouble for expressing anger in safe ways, as it is a normal feeling related to loss.

- Try and make the environment as safe as possible for your child to feel they can allow the anger out – this can include choosing the right time, a relaxing room in the house, over a weekend or late afternoon when the child is not tired, or allowing them a cuddly toy with them, or even a friend if they would like company.

- It is best to use these exercises when you have already seen some signs of anger in a child who may therefore need some guidance and support on how to express it safely. This is not what is normally known as anger management, as it is enabling anger rather than managing it.

- Each activity has specific guidance notes. Read these to choose which activity is best at different stages and with different groups or individual children.

Anger
Activity 4
Drawing My Anger

Guidance notes

👐 This activity enables a child who has experienced loss to accept this feeling, and to find a safe, contained way to express it.

👐 It can reassure the child that their feeling of anger will not always be there, is a result of their experience of loss, and that they will not be rejected if they feel anger.

Materials

👐 Copies of Drawing My Anger Worksheet, at least two for each child

👐 Coloured pens, pencils or crayons

Preparation

The exercise is suitable for individual children and groups. Prepare the children by talking about feelings related to loss and by describing anger. Describe the Drawing My Anger Worksheet as a page for putting your anger into the middle of the shape in whichever way you like: using words, pictures, colours, scribbles, memories. Remind them that although they can express their anger in this way, they cannot allow it to get out of control as the rules of behaviour are still the same.

What to do

1 Help the children to first think about what it is that makes them angry at the moment.

2 When they are ready, they can then draw or write about that in the centre of the shape.

3 Remind them there is no right and wrong, and that probably everyone in the room will have something different that makes them feel angry.

Page 1 of 2

4   Reassure children that it is acceptable to be seen throwing something in a bin, and tearing up the piece of paper when they have filled in the shape.

5   Ask if the child/children would like to do the exercise more than once.

Monitor carefully any child who may become out of control. For this reason, it can be helpful to have a few extra hands for support, particularly in a classroom setting. A small group is less demanding when using this exercise and individual children will gain greatly from the support of doing this exercise and the freedom that comes with allowing it.

Page 2 of 2

Drawing My Anger Worksheet

Anger is a normal feeling when someone close to you has died or gone away.

This activity will help you let it out safely so you do not hurt yourself or anyone else.

✋ Write or draw something in the shape that makes you feel angry. It can be something about what is happening, or simply a word.

✋ Colour over it with a red or black pen until you cannot see it any more, then screw it up, throw it in the bin and let some of the anger out.

✋ Do this as many times as you need to. You can also tear the page up and throw it in the bin as many times as you want.

✋ Tell someone you are doing this so they understand how you feel.

✋ You can use this page as many times as you want; your teacher will give you more copies.

Anger
Activity 5
The Shape of My Anger

Guidance notes

✍ This exercise is a physical means of letting out anger safely.

✍ Using Play-Doh® allows a child experiencing loss to use their positive creative talents, whilst acknowledging the difficult feeling of anger at the same time.

When children feel anger after a loss, it is often shown physically in their posture or their actions, such as hitting out, fidgeting, or being tense. As it is not acceptable for children to show their anger in ways that are destructive or damaging, particularly in a classroom, it can be helpful to provide physical ways to release anger. This can halt an accumulation of the feeling during the process of loss.

Materials

✍ Copies of The Shape of My Anger Worksheet, two for each child

✍ Play-Doh® in different colours

✍ Safe board or table to use as a surface for working the Play-Doh®

Preparation

Choose how to use this exercise. It can be used individually if a child is having problems with holding their anger in; alternatively it can be used in small groups to help children share their anger shapes together. In this way they can learn to support each other and to understand that it is acceptable to show anger, but not to take it out on each other.

Page 1 of 2

What to do

1 Give each child a copy of The Shape of My Anger Worksheet and a lump of Play-Doh® in any colour; ask them to only use their own piece of Play-Doh®.

2 Ask the children to remember when they have been angry recently or in the past.

3 Ask them to make a shape that seems to describe their anger.

4 Remind them not to copy anyone else: each person's shape of anger is different.

5 They can make as many shapes as they like, then destroy them and make more with the same lump of Play-Doh®.

6 When they are ready, help them to decide a final shape that represents their anger.

The room will probably be very loud and busy while they are doing this, because anger is an energetic emotion and will generate energy. Make sure that the children know this is acceptable within the rules of the group/classroom/home.

The Shape of My Anger Worksheet

- Hold a lump of Play-Doh® and make sure it is soft.

- Make the Play-Doh® into a shape that looks like your anger. It could look something like one of these shapes below or be completely different – you choose what it looks like.

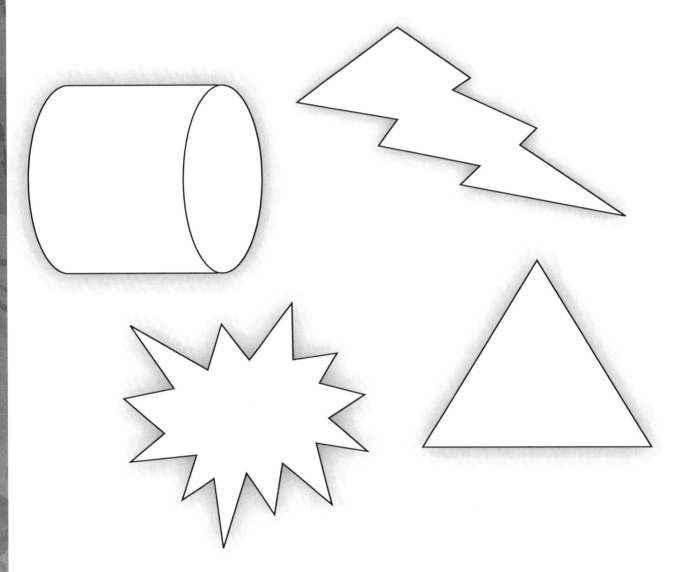

- Squeeze, pull and punch your shape, so that some of the anger is squeezed out.

- You can make two or more shapes one after another, squeezing each time. Do this until it feels you have no more anger to squeeze out for now.

- You can do this again if it helps to release some of your anger.

Anger
Activity 6
Angry Monsters

Guidance notes

🖐 The Angry Monsters activity is a great way for a child to draw what they think an angry monster looks like without associating it with themselves.

🖐 It allows a child to pretend to be a monster for a short time, because when children become really angry it could be said that their anger becomes like a monster.

🖐 Using their imagination, children can explore anger safely.

It is important for children to understand that anger is a part of all our lives, including when a loss has happened, but that sometimes when you are angry it can feel like the anger is a monster. Be sure that children understand that because you feel angry does not mean that you *are* a monster. Be aware that some children will be afraid of monsters, however, so encourage them to think of this as an exercise in imagination and make-believe, not as something real.

Materials

🖐 A copy of the Angry Monsters Worksheet for each child

🖐 Coloured pens, pencils or crayons

Preparation

This exercise works better with groups than individuals. Ask children what they think of monsters. Ask them if they think monsters ever get angry and allow them to discuss this. Describe the exercise as one in which they can imagine a monster that gets as angry as they want. Remember that some children will not want the monster to be very angry as that can be scary. Reassure them that their monster can be as angry as they wish it to be.

Page 1 of 2

What to do

1 Give each of the children a copy of the Angry Monsters Worksheet and tell them to start drawing the monster they have imagined.

2 When they have drawn their monster, place all the pictures on a wall and call it the 'Angry Monsters Wall'.

3 Can they decide which is the best and angriest monster in the group?

Check if any of the children are afraid of the monsters or the pictures. If this is the case, it is important to follow this exercise with a happy monster exercise (see Activities 7 & 8), to balance the feelings. Certain children can be very afraid either of their own potential for anger or that of others. Others love to be afraid or are not afraid at all.

Angry Monsters Worksheet

The Angry Monster

Imagine there is an angry monster somewhere in the world. What might it look like: what colour is it, what shape feet and hands will it have? Use your imagination as much as you can and draw your angry monster.

Anger

Activity 7

Monster Stories

Guidance notes

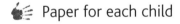 These stories are to help children make friends with the 'monsters' within themselves.

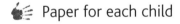 By thinking of endings for the stories and starting to tell a story of their own, children can begin to make sense of the internal monsters that sometimes haunt them.

The monsters in these activities are obviously symbolic of the things inside children that are scary, and sometimes feelings such as anger and fear can be very scary. Children experiencing loss in particular may have these internal fears. Reassure the children that if they become scared at any point during the activity they must ask for help and not continue with the story.

Children of primary age have a vivid imagination and the younger ages may have some difficulty if they are very impressionable, but the stories can be used for them to exercise their imagination in order to allow the monsters to find their rightful place in their minds. Ensure there are enough adult supporters to help if a child becomes scared as a result of talk about monsters. It may be that some of the children have a very real fear of them for some reason that is yet unknown. As this is the age when night lights are still important, be aware that the stories may be more suited to older age groups.

Materials

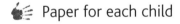 Paper for each child

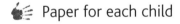 Coloured pens, pencils or crayons

 Monster Stories Worksheet

Preparation

This can be a group or an individual exercise. Introduce the stories as a fun exercise in making up tales to do with monsters in which they will be able to choose the ending of the story themselves.

Page 1 of 2

As Activity 6 was about the angry monster, the children may associate monsters only with anger, so the stories in this activity are to help them understand that monsters can be related to many feelings. Allow the children to discuss in the class, before the exercise, how monsters may behave and then how the stories may end.

Ask the children if they can think of other stories that have monsters in them. Some children may only remember horror stories, and some funny stories. There are no right or wrong endings to these stories, but do monitor how the stories proceed. If you think an ending is particularly bad or unhelpful, try and ask other children how they would make it different.

What to do

1 Read a story from the Monster Stories Worksheet and give each child time to write their own ending.
2 Then allow a group of children to choose one ending they particularly like, and ask if they would like to act it out or tell it to the whole class.
3 A good way to complete this exercise would be for each child to do a drawing of their favourite story and put these up on the wall as monster stories.

Monster Stories Worksheet

1   Once upon a time there was a land full of monsters. They were of all kinds: happy, sad, frightened, worried, crazy, mad, angry and even married. One day an angry monster met a happy monster ... What happened next and how did it end?

2   There was a family of monsters living in the woods. Mum and dad monster were happy, but their son was quite angry. He often went into the wood to chop the trees down, but did not want to use the wood. That was stupid because trees are very precious, but he did it because he was angry. One day mum monster said she had had enough, and said that if he chopped down one more tree she would send him away ... What happened next and how did it end?

3   In a world with no other monsters, monster Fred felt all alone. He had no one to help him, no one to show him how to live, no one to show him what to do when he grew up, and no one to help him when he felt sad and angry. He had been alone for so long that he wondered if he would ever meet anyone in the world who understood him. Then one day he went to his favourite place in the whole wide world and standing there was ... Complete this story.

4   Tom and Alice were two children who lived happily in a big house with their parents and pets. They had never met a monster and really they did not want to. They may have been frightened of meeting one, much like they would have been frightened if they met a dragon. But a part of them was curious, because they had heard that sometimes monsters crept out of the wood at night and could be seen playing in the moonlight. So they decided to stay up one night and find out ... What happened next and how did it end?

Page 1 of 2

5 Do you believe in monsters? Because I do. They have a way of sneaking up on you when you least expect it. They are hiding in the most unexpected places, like the supermarket aisles or in dark corners. Most of the time these monsters are not scary, because once you show them the light, they are so happy that they shrink to small monster size and jump about as if they never see daylight. Which of course they do not usually. So one day I decided to see if I could shake out all the monsters in my house so I never had to be afraid again ... What happened next and how does it end?

Anger

Activity 8

Monster Moves

Guidance notes

 This exercise allows children to express their anger in a safe way by dramatising it as a monster.

Materials

 Copies of Monster Moves Worksheet for each child

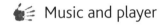 Music and player

Whistle or bell for signal

Preparation

Ensure the children know that this is a fun exercise to do with monsters and allow them the space and time to enjoy this. Anger can be fun!

Use a room such as a gym, hall or other large area that has lots of space for children to move around and make noise; give the children the time and space to prepare for the exercise by doing warm-up exercises first, such as shaking or moving the body freely.

What to do

1 Remind them at the beginning that they must watch you to make sure they stop when you say, as the room could become very loud at times.

2 It is usually best to finish with a calming exercise such as the breathing exercise on the Calming Breaths Worksheet (Activity 9).

3 If you prefer to control the noise levels of the room, choose a piece of music that could be called 'loud monster' music, and turn this up when the children begin to act out their monsters.

4 If you use music, do find a second piece of music for the happy monster acting; when you want the children to change roles, give your signal or turn off the 'loud monster' music and switch to the 'happy monster' music.

5 Always end the session with a shake-out of arms and legs, so that the children do not take the feelings they have been dramatising back into the classroom or away with them to lunch.

6 When you finish the session, you could go back to the classroom and give each child the chance to draw the monster that they acted out. The drawings could then be displayed on the wall.

Page 2 of 2

Monster Moves Worksheet

Instructions

1 Remember to watch and listen to your teacher or group leader whatever she wants you to, as this exercise can be very noisy at times.

2 You are going to pretend to be a monster in a strange world. Imagine that this monster is huge, ugly and ready to be very angry.

3 Imagine what colour you are, what voice you might have, and how you walk.

4 Begin by walking around the room, using the monster walk you have decided on.

5 When you are ready, use the rest of your body and see if you can walk and move your body as a monster.

6 Then, when you are ready, use your voice and see if you can make your voice an angry voice.

7 The room will be noisy, so make sure you look at your teacher from time to time to see if they want you to do something different.

8 What does it feel like to be angry as a monster? Is your body feeling strong or weak?

9 At the signal or change in music, you should stop, absolutely still, on one spot – and shake that monster away. As you are standing there, begin to find a different monster inside of you.

10 This time, find the happy monster. How does it walk and move?

11 Imagine what colour you are and what voice you might have.

Page 1 of 2

12 When you are ready, walk and move as the happy monster.

13 For a few minutes let the happy monster talk as well.

14 Then at the signal stop, absolutely still, on one spot again.

15 Do a final shake-up to make sure you shake out all the monster feelings inside you.

16 Come back to the group and talk with your teacher and think about what it was like to be a monster for a short time.

Anger
Activity 9
Calming Breaths

Guidance notes

👏 This exercise is about anger management.

👏 It aims to give a child the tools to choose when and how to be angry, by using breath control and counting to manage their feelings.

Sometimes it is important for a child to calm down if their expression of anger becomes out of control, and particularly if they are in danger of either hurting themself or someone else. Using their breath is one of the best ways to teach a child how to manage their anger.

Although this is an exercise for calming down, it is best introduced before a child loses control, since the more a child is prepared for this, the better they can manage if they do then become out of control with their anger.

Preparation

The exercise can be used with an individual child or with groups of children. Prepare the children by describing the exercise as one to do with breath and anger. Make sure that children have some time to use this exercise properly.

When working with groups of children, make sure the children have space (a room where they can stand and move around), and direct them to keep at a fingertips-stretched distance from each other. Children can also sit at their desks to do this exercise although this would make less impact on them if it were part of a lesson.

Calming Breaths Worksheet

Breath Control Instructions

👏 Find a space in the room where you can be comfortable

👏 Follow the instructions you are given.

👏 Imagine you are feeling angry. You could even think of something that makes you feel angry, but not too angry.

👏 Count from one to ten, taking in a big breath as you do. If one breath is not enough time for each count, take a second 'in' breath.

👏 Your teacher will help you by counting from one to ten for you.

👏 Then slowly let out your breath, counting backwards from ten to one. Your teacher will again help you by counting from ten back to one. At one, you should be more relaxed and much calmer. Again, if you need more than one breath, take a second 'out' breath.

👏 Feel your body as much calmer and check if the feeling of anger you began with is reduced.

👏 This can be done more than once.

👏 Once you have done this, whenever you feel strong anger coming on that is almost too strong for you to control, you can use this exercise to help calm it down. It does not push your anger away, but it calms it down so you can choose how to express it safely.

Activities for Specific Feelings
Activities 10–14: Sadness

Guidance notes

Feeling sad is very normal when a child has experienced a loss, whatever the cause. Showing sad feelings may or may not be normal to them, and this will depend on many things, including how a family shows feelings, their temperament, the nature of the loss, and their previous experience of life and other losses.

Sometimes children confuse sad feelings with angry feelings. They can also hide their sad feelings if they think the adults in their family are too sad themselves.

At school children may find it hard to be sad when all their friends are being happy and normal. Some children will enjoy school as they can forget how sad they feel, others will feel it as a pressure on them to pretend they are feeling normal.

However, it is best for children who do feel sad at school to have somewhere they can go when they feel too sad to join in with daily activities, whether it is a quiet place in school, or even to return home.

Focusing on sad feelings can therefore be difficult at certain stages of a loss, but acknowledging that sadness is a part of loss is very important.

Guidance for professionals

- Decide if the children will be doing individual or group activities.
- Ensure that any particularly vulnerable children are supported, either by a particular adult or a close friend.
- Prepare the children by discussing feelings generally, including sadness.
- If offering an individual exercise for a child, make sure they are in a safe place where they can relax and, if necessary, show their feelings by crying. This can be a room used for support such as a quiet library area or other. It is usually best for it to be separate from other children, unless there are a few children experiencing the same feelings of loss.
- If offering a group exercise, remind the children that they are there to support each other and that it is important to help each other, as being sad is hard.

Page 1 of 2

- Make sure there is enough time for the exercise and for the possibility that some children will be more affected than others.

- At the end of sad exercises, it can be helpful for there to be a relaxing activity, perhaps a more active exercise such as PE, or a lunchtime so that children who have been deeply affected can recover before proper lessons begin again.

Guidance for parents and carers

- Offering support for children who are sad can be difficult when you are parents and carers who are yourselves sad. However it can be very encouraging for children to know that, despite your own pain, you care about how they feel enough to support them.

- Therefore make sure you feel strong enough to do these exercises. If you are not, allow someone else less involved to support your child in this way, such as the school professionals or another close relative.

- Provide a quiet space and a quiet time to allow for your child to draw and talk more about their sadness.

- Check if they feel fine about showing you their feelings at this time. Sometimes children really want to protect those around them and not show their true feelings if it upsets their relatives.

- Reassure your child that it is fine to show you their strong feelings, and that if you cry it is because you are also sad. Crying in front of them encourages them to know that their own feelings are normal too.

- Use the exercises to help your child to think of ways they show their sad feelings, as well as some of the ways they can use to make their sad feelings better. In this way you can continue the dialogue about how to support them in their sadness.

Page 2 of 2

Sadness

Activity 10

Sad Circles

Guidance notes

 This exercise is to enable a child to begin to share some of the thoughts or memories of what makes them feel sad.

 The child is asked to consider ways that this feeling can be supported. Some children may not know what it is that helps them, and these children may need suggestions from an adult.

 The child will also be reminded that their sad feelings will come and go.

Materials

 Paper

 Writing pencils or pens

Preparation

This exercise is often better for individual use or for a small select group to support each other. Choose the environment carefully, ensuring that any child doing this exercise is not on their own. Having both an adult and some friends nearby is important so that any feelings that emerge can be shared.

What to do

1 Tell the child that they can ask for anything at any time while they are doing this exercise, as it is to help them with their feelings.

2 Encourage the child to be as honest as they can be, as this is helpful for them.

Page 1 of 2

3 Give the children the ground rule that if one of them becomes upset during the exercise, they can allow their friend to be upset and to be comforted, either by one of the other children or by an adult.

4 It is important when the exercise is finished to change the mood back to being happy, so that the feelings of sadness are released. Children need to know that they do not need to be sad all the time; as children dip into and out of feelings all the time, particularly when they experience loss, this is important. This can be simply done by perhaps doing the exercise before playtime, or finishing with one of the happy exercises.

Page 2 of 2

Sad Circles Worksheet

Feeling sad is normal when you have lost someone close to you. It is also OK to forget to be sad at times.

Write or draw three things in the circles that make you feel sad at this time or have made you feel sad in the past. There are no right or wrong things to write or draw, and the thing can be as small or as big as you like.

Now, in the boxes, write or draw three things that can help you or have helped you in the past, when you feel sad. Some of them might be in this list:

- Crying

- Listening to sad music

- Telling someone how you feel

- Looking at a sad picture

- Getting a cuddle from someone you trust

- Forgetting to be sad for five minutes when the sun comes out

- Listening to happy music

Remember that being sad is OK and being happy is OK too.

Page 1 of 2

Sad Circles

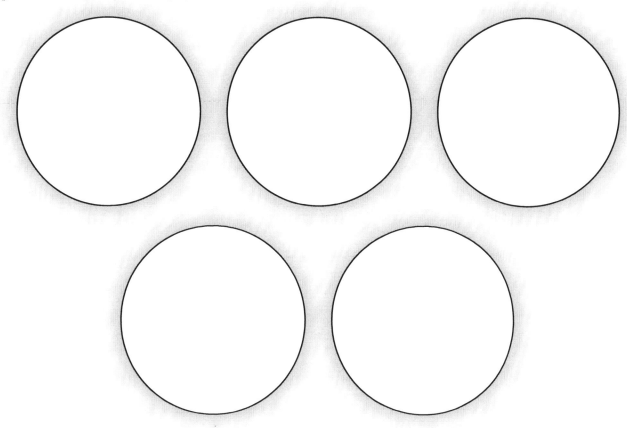

Helpful Boxes

Page 2 of 2

Sadness

Activity 11

Sad Colours – Happy Colours

Guidance notes

👐 This exercise allows children to experiment with colours and how they represent the feelings inside them.

👐 Children always enjoy doing this exercise, because there is something magical about layers of colours and revealing what is beneath.

👐 This exercise does not take the sadness away, but it helps children to understand that it is possible to be happy as well as sad.

Materials

👐 A copy of Sad Colours – Happy Colours Worksheet for each child

👐 Good quality wax crayons: oil pastel crayons are excellent for this exercise as they are coloured deeply and can be layered onto the paper easily

👐 Pens or pencils to draw the squiggly lines on top of the wax crayon colour

---

Preparation

This is an exercise suitable for both groups and individual children. An excellent way to introduce it is to ask a child or children to remember a colour that is related to their loss. This can be easier for some children than choosing a colour to represent sadness. It is also possible to ask a child to close their eyes and imagine a colour for 'sad' and 'happy'. Nearly all children will choose a colour quickly this way.

Page 1 of 2

What to do

1 Give the children clear instructions for each section of the exercise and have helpers nearby so that a group of children can do this together.

2 Allow them to choose first one colour, then another, using one of the methods above.

3 The children may want to talk about why they chose certain colours. Children who have been bereaved or have experienced a loss will often remember the favourite colour of their loved one, or the 'colour' of a particular experience they shared together.

4 It does not matter if the child does not fully understand the meaning behind the exercise, as this form of exercise can be therapeutic in itself.

5 After this exercise, always check how the child or children are feeling so that they can talk about their own sadness or share some memories if they need to.

Sad Colours – Happy Colours Worksheet

1   Choose a colour for your sad feeling, if necessary with the help of your teacher.

2   Then colour in the first square with this colour using a wax crayon.

3   Now choose a colour for your happy feeling.

4   Colour over the top of the first colour completely. Make sure no colour is showing through.

5   Using the end of a pen or pencil, draw a picture or squiggle some lines on the crayon so that the first colour shows through the second layer. You can draw what you want on the wax colour.

6   This is how feeling sad can sometimes feel – always there underneath, but you can hide it sometimes.

7   When you are ready, use the second square to do the opposite colours.

8   Start with the colour for happy in the second square.

9   Then add on top the colour for the sad feeling, covering it completely.

10 Then, using a pen or pencil again, draw a design on the wax colour. Draw whatever you like.

11 This is what it feels like when the sad feeling is getting smaller and the happy feelings are showing up again.

Sometimes the sad feeling will be underneath, and sometimes the happy feeling will be underneath, when you have experienced losing someone important to you. There is no right and wrong way to feel.

Page 1 of 2

Box 1	Box 2
Sad Underneath	**Happy Underneath**
Happy on Top	**Sad on Top**

129

Sadness

Activity 12

Sad Self – Happy Self

Guidance notes

🖐 This exercise asks children to draw themselves looking sad and then looking happy.

🖐 It allows them to visualise themselves feeling different things.

🖐 They can begin to recognise that they may be happy outside, but inside they may be sad.

Materials

🖐 A copy of the Sad Self – Happy Self Worksheet for each child

🖐 Coloured pencils or crayons

Preparation

Ensure that any child who has experienced a recent loss is in a group of children who can support them if the feeling becomes bigger for a time. This is a good exercise to do in a small group or circle time, so that children can talk about how they feel while doing the exercise and what they may say.

What to do

🖐 Encourage the children to think of a time when they were sad and what they might have looked like when sad.

🖐 Show them with your posture, for example, what a sad person may look like – bending over, looking with little energy, withdrawn from the world with a very sad, turned-down expression on your face.

🖐 Then ask them to draw how they looked when they were sad either from memory, or what they saw you looking like if they cannot think of a time when they were sad.

Page 1 of 2

- While they are drawing, ask them when they may have felt this feeling, ready for when they are going to write in the speech bubble.

- Now ask them to think of a time when they were happy and what they might have looked like.

- Again show them how being happy may look in your posture, looking up and bright, full of energy and with a big smile.

- Then ask them to draw how they looked when they were happy or if they cannot think of their own experience of being happy, to draw how you look when being happy.

- Ask them if they can remember the last time they had this feeling.

- Now ask the children what might both the sad and happy person they have drawn might be saying to each other.

- Ask them to write this in the speech bubbles.

- Finally ask them if the happy or sad self has something particularly important to say now, and write this in the big speech bubble at the bottom..

- Remind them finally that it is acceptable to feel sad when something has happened such as a loss, but that it is also acceptable to be happy. And sometimes the happy person is the one showing even if inside them they are feeling sad.

Page 2 of 2

Sad Self - Happy Self Worksheet

👋 In box 1 draw yourself on a sad day. You can draw your whole body or just your face.

👋 In box 2 draw yourself on a happy day. You can draw your whole body or just your face.

👋 Colour the pictures in the way you like – make them as complicated or as simple as you like.

👋 Now, in the speech bubbles above each box, give each picture something to say to the other.

👋 What will your sad self say?

👋 What will your happy self say?

👋 Finish by using the last big balloon under boxes to let your sad or happy self say something that is important for you at the moment.

👋 Remember, if you ever feel sad, to let your sad self talk out so your happy self can hear.

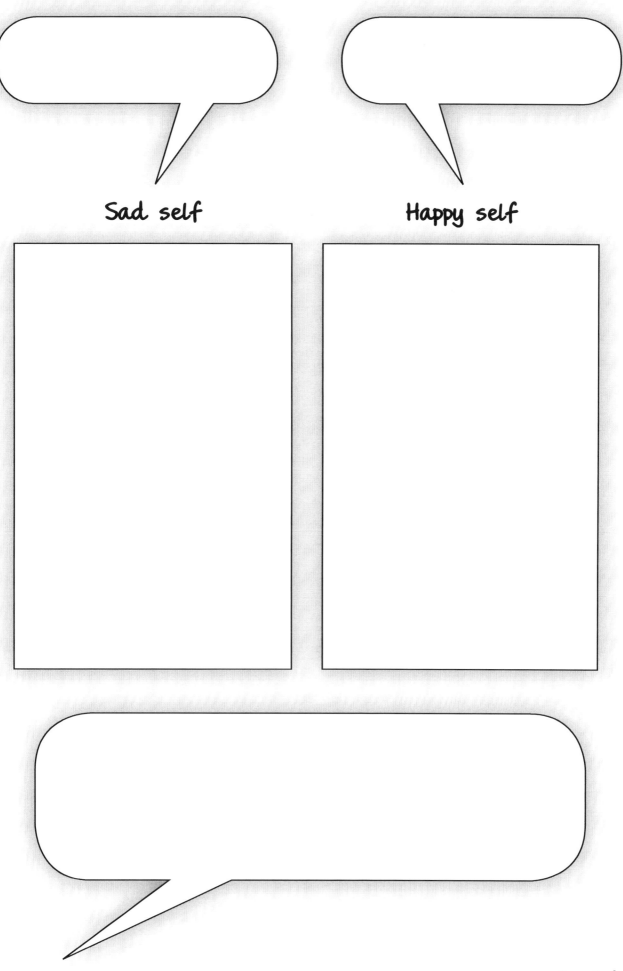

Sad self

Happy self

Page 2 of 2

Sadness

Activity 13

Sadness Collage

Guidance notes

👏 In this activity the children will make a collage of images and craft materials that represent, for them, the sad part of themselves.

👏 Each child will have their own experience of being sad. By making a collage of this, the sad feelings become more acceptable, while still being the focus.

👏 Making art that relates to their feelings is an important way children can accept and express their feelings.

Materials

👏 A Sadness Collage Worksheet for each child

👏 A large piece of cartridge paper for each child

👏 Postcards and pictures from magazines (images from films or with a musical theme, as well as people, animals, nature, abstract pictures, etc.)

👏 Various art and craft materials: felt, tissue paper, coloured card, coloured paper and glitter (which can be very messy)

👏 Aprons to protect clothes

👏 Safety scissors

👏 Glue

Preparation

This exercise is often better for individual use or for a small, select group that can support individuals within the group. Ensure that there are also enough staff to offer support, both practically and emotionally, as needed. This exercise will probably end up being a fun exercise, which is a good way to let out the sad feelings.

What to do

1 Give each child a large piece of cartridge paper.

2 Describe the activity as one in which they are going to make a work of art which they can call 'sad' at the end. The artwork will be their own idea of what sad means to them.

3 Remind the children there is no right and wrong, and if a child becomes particularly sad during that activity that they should ask for help from someone nearby who they trust.

4 When the children have made their collages, place them up on the wall or somewhere to display them.

5 Ask them if they feel the sad feeling when they look at their artwork. They may not, which is fine.

6 Ask each child then to shake out any sad feelings they have left in their body, so that they can move on to the next activity/lesson of the day without any leftover sadness inside them.

Sad Collage Worksheet

Make a Collage

- On the table are lots of pictures, card, paper, and other bits that you can use.

- You are going to make a collage to show how you feel when you feel sad. You can choose anything on the table.

- A collage is a mix of different materials all put together on one sheet of paper to make a work of art. This is going to be your work of art on Sad.

- When making a collage, it is best to start with a few basic pictures or materials and add to them slowly.

- Think about what pictures and colours are most sad for you.

- Only use small amounts of glue, and only choose the pictures and materials and colours that are right for you.

- Each person's picture will be different. This is fine, because each person's experience of being sad is different too. There is no right and wrong.

- While you are making your picture, think of anything that has made you sad, so that your artwork really is about being sad.

At the end, we will make sure we make ourselves happy again, as being sad all the time is not right.

Sadness

Activity 14
Sad Face or Happy Face

Guidance notes

🖐 This exercise uses clay to allow a child to express their feelings, since clay is a medium that most children love to use.

Materials

🖐 A Sad Face or Happy Face Worksheet for each child

🖐 A lump of clay (soft enough to use) for each child

🖐 Boards on which to work the clay

🖐 Aprons

Preparation

As clay is a messy activity, this activity can only be done in an environment where being messy is acceptable. If the classroom is not suitable, you can use Play-Doh® or Plasticine® instead, although they tend not to be as satisfying and models cannot be kept afterwards.

What to do

Give children enough time to make the faces in the exercise and offer help if they are not sure how to make a face. Some older children will want to add extra features like hair and ears. If possible, allow them to keep the face at the end.

Sad Face or Happy Face Worksheet

· 🖐 Hold your piece of clay or Play-Doh® in your hands and start to make a ball with it. Make it as round as you can.

🖐 When you are ready, make a sad face on this ball – make it as sad as you like. Does it look sad to you?

🖐 Then, turn the sad face around and make a happy face on the back. Make it as happy as you can. Does it look happy to you?

🖐 You now have a sad and a happy face all in one.

🖐 Remember that sometimes, when you look sad, behind that is a happy face.

🖐 And the opposite, sometimes when you look happy, behind that is a sad face.

Do any of you remember a time when you have shown one face but had another behind it?

Activities for Specific Feelings
Activities 15-18: Worries

Guidance notes

Children who are bereaved or have experienced a loss from another cause often have worries and concerns. Sometimes these worries are small and a child can be easily reassured. At other times these worries are huge, or seem large to the child, and may need some time to resolve. The worries can be about many things:

🖐 They may be about the person the child has lost, such as why they went away and if the child is to blame for the person leaving.

🖐 They may be about what happens to them, the child, after the loss: are they going to have to move house or to live with someone else?

🖐 They may even be worries – after a particularly distressing bereavement – about whether they are going to die themselves.

One of the ways worries can be helped is by sharing them. A child who has been bereaved may not have had an opportunity to tell someone about their worries (either before or after their loss), due to the distress or other events connected with the loss. A child who has been bereaved by complicated causes such as suicide or murder will probably have more serious worries due to the nature of the loss. Other losses such as divorce or moving house can cause children to worry, for example, about their relatives, or even their siblings.

Often children do not know how to share their worries or are ashamed to have them. They may be able to share them with a beloved pet or a toy, but often not with an adult who can help. They may do this to protect the adults, or because they believe they have done something wrong and should try and manage without telling adults.

🖐 It is important to have a teacher, teaching assistant or other adult close by so that any child who wishes to share a worry is able to do so safely as a result of these exercises.

🖐 Give the child instructions for each stage of the exercises and explain that these are exercises to allow any worries to get smaller.

🖐 Always ask the children at the end of an exercise if there is anything they would like to say about the exercise or the worries.

Worries
Activity 15
Shrinking Worries

Guidance notes

✋ This exercise uses colour and imagination to help a child begin to 'shrink' their worry.

✋ Since most children naturally think in colours and shapes, they find this an easy way to think about their worries.

Materials

✋ Shrinking Worries Worksheet, at least one copy for each child

✋ Coloured pencils or crayons

Preparation

Ensure that all the children are in groups in which they feel safe, or are on their own in a safe place. Begin by talking generally about worries to the children, asking if children have had worries in their lives. Mention that it can be important to share worries, or to do something to help them become smaller, as children with worries are not always so happy.

What to do

1 Ask the children to write down or draw one or more worries in Box 1 on the Worksheet. Remind them that there is no right or wrong in this exercise, and that it is best not to copy anyone else, as each person may have their own worry.

2 Lead them into a small quiet time, in which they close their eyes, relax, and think about the worry in Box 1. Ask them to think of a colour that they think can help this worry. Then guide them to draw this colour in Box 2. Allow them to take as long as they want over this, as it can really help their worry.

Page 1 of 2

3 Then ask them to use Box 3 and to put any feelings about the worry that have not changed as a result of drawing the helpful colour in Box 2.

4 This exercise can be repeated on a new Worksheet, but doing it just once may be enough for most children.

It may be helpful to check if, at the end of the exercise, some of the children want to tell what their worry was and what colour helped them. Remind them that once they have used this exercise, they can use this colour or other colours whenever they have a worry that is bothering them.

It is also important to remind the children that, when they are ready, sharing their worry with someone usually helps to shrink it, or to manage it. If they are unsure who to share their worry with, ask if they would normally tell someone in their family or someone special at school, such as their teacher or teaching assistant, or the lunchtime supervisor.

Shrinking Worries Worksheet

Everybody has worries sometimes, and when you lose someone close to you the worries can seem huge. It is important to tell someone so they can help you, but you can use this page to help you work out which worries you might need to share and which ones you do not need any more.

1 Write about or draw a worry in Box 1. You can use words, a shape or a picture. You can fill in the whole box.

2 Close your eyes, relax a moment, and think of a colour that helps with the feeling of having this worry.

3 Put this colour in Box 2, colouring it as much as you want. As you colour it, feel the colour shrinking the worry.

4 Use Box 3 to write or draw any changes you feel about the worry after thinking of the colour.

5 Decide if this worry needs to be shared with an adult nearby.

6 You can do this exercise again if you have more than one worry. The Worksheet gives space for up to three worries.

7 Ask a teacher for more worksheets if you have more than three worries.

Remember that after this exercise you can decide if you would like to share one or more of your worries with someone nearby.

Box 1 MY WORRY	Box 2 HELPING COLOUR	Box 3 ANY CHANGES

Worries

Activity 16

How Big is My Worry?

Guidance notes

A child who has experienced loss may have worries that seem bigger than they actually are and might be reluctant to share these. In this exercise the child uses simple art shapes to begin to talk about their worries and is given the opportunity to:

🖐 Write about the worry;

🖐 Decide how big they think it is;

🖐 Think about what might help to make it smaller.

Materials

🖐 A copy of the How Big is My Worry? Worksheet for each child

🖐 Coloured pencils or crayons

What to do

1 Talk the child or children through the exercise first, so that they know what is expected of them.

2 Be clear that they are allowed to fill in each square of the Worksheet in exactly the way they want.

3 Never force a child with worries to share them, because their worries may be about things they have been asked to keep secret.

4 If a child begins to write or tell about serious worries, use your experience and expertise to decide how important it is to inform others and how to keep the child safe.

5 It is important to tell children that if they get upset at any time they should tell a teacher or other adult.

How Big is My Worry? Worksheet

On this Worksheet, you will be able to write about a worry, and choose how big it feels to you. If you don't have any worries, it is not the right activity for you and you don't need to do it.

1 Choose a shape from the page of worry shapes or make up your own worry shape.

2 Next, draw this shape in the box.

3 Write down what you think this worry is about.

4 Decide if your worry is big or small and circle the right word.

5 Next, put a cross next to 1, 2, 3, 4 or 5 to show just how big or small this worry is to you now (5 is the biggest worry and 1 is the smallest worry).

6 Next, write down what you think will help with your worry.

7 Can you draw this shape smaller in the next box to make it shrink? Sometimes just telling someone or writing it down makes a worry feel smaller.

8 Talk to a teacher about your worries if you need to after doing this activity.

Page 1 of 3

This is my worry about _____

_____

It feels SMALL / BIG

1 _____ 2 _____ 3 _____ 4 _____ 5 _____

What can help you make this worry smaller? _____

_____

Draw the worry shape you put in the first box smaller if you feel you can.

Worry Shapes

Page 3 of 3

Worries

Activity 17

Dealing with Worries

Guidance notes

This exercise offers an easy way to identify if a child needs extra help with worries by offering the child a choice of answers to three simple questions:

1 What would they do if they were worried?
2 Who would they tell if they were worried?
3 What do they need if they are worried?

Introduce this exercise by saying all children have worries sometimes, but there are lots of different ways to deal with them and lots of different ways a child can be helped.

Dealing with Worries Worksheet

When I have worries I can tell:

- [ ] my parent
- [ ] my teacher
- [ ] my carer
- [ ] my pet
- [ ] my friends
- [ ] my friends on computer

- [ ] my counsellor
- [ ] my play therapist
- [ ] my teaching assistant
- [ ] my toy
- [ ] no one
- [ ] other _____

When I have worries I may:

- [ ] tell someone
- [ ] watch television
- [ ] go and play outside
- [ ] play computer games
- [ ] play music
- [ ] do nothing

- [ ] sit and read
- [ ] sit quietly and speak to no one
- [ ] go on the computer
- [ ] do sports, such as football
- [ ] write or draw
- [ ] other _____

When I have worries I need:

- [ ] someone to talk to
- [ ] to be left alone
- [ ] someone to give me a cuddle
- [ ] someone to help me forget
- [ ] a warm drink
- [ ] a nice meal

- [ ] to sleep
- [ ] to go out and play
- [ ] help
- [ ] to know I am not to blame
- [ ] to cuddle my cat/dog/pet
- [ ] my family all around me

Remember to tell a teacher or your parent or other adult if your worries are too big to keep to yourself.

Worries

Activity 18

Sharing Worries

Guidance notes

✋ This exercise uses art materials to help a child express their worries.

Materials

✋ A copy of the Sharing Worries Worksheet for each child

✋ Play-Doh®

✋ Boards on which to work the Play-Doh®

✋ Play-Doh® tools

Preparation

Explain that all worries dislike seeing daylight and dislike someone sharing them, because this makes them shrink. Therefore everyone is going to make a worry and show it to someone else so that the worry will shrink almost to nothing. Tell the children that making their worry into a shape could be fun.

What to do

1 Encourage the children to make their worry any shape they like.

2 If they do not have a worry, they can just make a shape and share it.

3 When they have made the shape, ask them who they would like to show their shape to. They do not have to tell the person their worry, only the *shape* of their worry. This is very important, because the children may not feel ready to share some of their worries with another person, but this will help them prepare.

4 Do encourage them to share the shape, even if just with one other child on their table.

5 They will then make the worry shape smaller and smaller until it disappears.

Sharing Worries Worksheet

- Hold your Play-Doh® in your hands.

- Think of a worry you have had recently, maybe something you are still worried about or one from the past that you are nearly able to finish worrying about.

- Make a shape for this worry. It can be any shape you like – it is just your shape of your worry. It can be round, square, oblong, a bowl shape, a spiky shape, a sausage shape. Anything you choose.

- When you have made this shape, think who you would like to show this shape to. Remember – worries do not like to be shared, because then they shrink and can even disappear. So you can share your worry shape with someone to help it shrink. If you want, you can share the worry too, not just the shape. **But you do not have to share the worry with anyone.** Showing the shape is enough.

- Now show the shape to a teacher, a teaching assistant, or someone else.

- If anyone wants to share their shape with the whole class, your teacher will get you to come to the front of the class to show everybody.

- When you have either showed your shape to everyone or to one person, make your shape smaller. Because your shape has been shared, it is now a smaller worry.

- How small does it need to be? Can it shrink completely yet or is it just a bit smaller?

- What would it take to make it even smaller still? If you need to share it again to shrink it more, you can do this now. Tell your teacher if you want to do this.

- When you are ready, make the shape so small that you can hardly see it any more – and make it back into a lump of Play-Doh®, not a worry shape.

- Congratulations, you have now successfully shrunk a worry!

- If you find it impossible to shrink this worry, it probably means that this is a worry that has to be shared fully with someone safe who can help you.

Activities for Specific Feelings
Activity 19
Feeling Guilty

Guidance notes

This exercise allows a child to remove feelings of guilt safely by drawing or writing what it is they feel responsible for, and then getting rid of it.

All children who are bereaved have a tendency to blame themselves sometimes. Guilt is also a normal emotion for adults when someone dies. Helping children to recognise that these feelings are not ones they should hang onto, and that they should tell someone if they do feel they are to blame, is very important in bereavement support.

Materials

A Feeling Guilty Worksheet for each child

Coloured pens and pencils

Rubbish bin

What to Do

1 Explain that often children feel to blame if someone has died or gone away. This is known as feeling guilty.

2 They should write their feelings of being to blame in the box on the Worksheet.

3 Then they will colour over the top of the guilty feelings and make them go away.

4 Now they can get rid of the feelings by tearing up the Worksheet and throwing it away.

5 Tell the children that it is fine to tear the page up; this is an unusual activity in the classroom and they may need your confirmation that you expect them to do this.

6 Give the children time to decide what to write or draw before they colour over it.

Feeling Guilty Worksheet

👏 Nothing you do can make someone die or leave, but sometimes it feels like you are to blame.

👏 This feeling is called feeling guilty and everyone who has lost someone has this feeling sometimes.

👏 Write down any feelings you have about being to blame in the box below.

👏 Then colour all over it with a colour that is bright and that you like. Cover up the writing completely.

👏 Now get rid of these feelings by tearing up the page and putting in the bin – This is where this type of feeling belongs.

It is not your fault!

Activities for Specific Feelings
Activities 20–22: Happiness

Guidance notes

🖐 The happiness activities enable a child to be reminded of being happy, especially if they have become stuck in one particular feeling.

Some children who are bereaved or who have experienced significant loss are unsure if it is acceptable to still be happy. Therefore children need to be encouraged to know it is fine to feel happy, and absolutely normal, and that they cannot be sad or angry all the time. Adults often find this hard, but dipping in and out of difficult feelings is a child's normal way of showing grief and loss.

Materials

🖐 Worksheets for each of the three exercises, one for each child

🖐 Paper

🖐 Coloured pencils or crayons

What to do

These pages can be used both with individual children and groups of children. All children need to remember the happy times they have had in their family.

1 The first exercise guides children to find three different ways that they feel happy. Give the child time to complete each section, so that they can think of the best ways they can find to feel happy. Give them the freedom to choose whether to write or to draw, as each child is different. Finally, encourage the child to keep this Worksheet if they are often not happy, so that it can help remind them what they need to think of in order to be happy.

2 The second exercise guides children to remember one particular feeling of being happy and to draw it large. They can then keep it to remind themselves if they have not been very happy recently.

3 The third exercise reminds children who have experienced a loss that although they have had a difficult time, either through someone dying or another form of loss, their family has had happy times and hopefully will again.

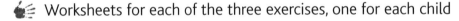

Happy
Activity 20
Ways to Feel Happy Worksheet

👆 What helps you to feel happy? It is very important to remember that it is OK to feel happy sometimes, even if something horrible has happened in your life and your family. Draw or write something in Box 1 that makes you laugh.

👆 Is there a place you go to that helps you feel happy? For example, the seaside, to a relative's house, an imaginary place. Draw or write it down in Box 2.

👆 Is there something special that helps keep you feeling happy? Or do you imagine doing something that makes you happy? Draw or write down what this is in Box 3.

Keep these pictures or writings to remind you that it is OK to be happy even when you have had a difficult experience, such as losing someone close to you.

Page 1 of 2

Ways to Feel Happy

1 What makes you laugh?

2 A place that makes you happy.

3 Something that helps you feel happy.

Page 2 of 2

Happy
Activity 21
My Happy Place Worksheet

Happy feelings come and go when you have experienced a person dying or leaving.

👆 Think of a time when you were happy recently. It could be at home, at school, with friends, doing an activity.

👆 Draw a picture of your happy self in that place, with those friends, doing that activity. Make it as large as you can – fill the whole page if you can.

👆 By doing this drawing, you are helping yourself to feel happy again.

👆 Keep this drawing by you. Every time you feel your happy feeling go and you need to feel happy again, look at this picture and it will help to remind you of being happy.

My Happy Place

Page 2 of 2

Happy
Activity 22
Happy Times Worksheet

Draw a picture of your family doing something fun together. Having fun with your family is important, even when you have all lost someone important to you.

Activities for Specific Feelings

Activities 23–24: Fear

Guidance notes

 These activities are to help children face their fears.

All children who experience loss and bereavement are afraid of something. It may be the dark, it may be losing one parent if they have lost one already, it may be that they are scared of ghosts, of dying, of losing their home, or their friends. Fear can be unknown or known, but it can be very disabling if it is not addressed. Children who experience loss become insecure, and their unknown and known fears will become manifest in behaviour such as clinging, crying and school refusal if they are not addressed.

Materials

 Fears Worksheets

 Writing pencils or pens

Preparation

Ensure children are in a safe place so that they can face some of their fears. This may involve being in a quiet room or corner with trusted adults, or near close friends. Create a calm atmosphere in which difficult feelings can be aired. Sometimes it is helpful for children to do this exercise on their own with a trusted adult just in case they become particularly upset.

Prepare the children by describing some of the feelings associated with loss, including being afraid of some things. Ask the children if there are things they are particularly afraid of. All of the children will have seen scary programmes on the television or frightening computer games, but not all of them will have experienced fear in own their lives. Those who have may need the support of children who have not.

Page 1 of 2

What to do

1 The first activity, Lighting Up Fears, allows a child to bring light to what can often be dark: mysterious and scary feelings of fear. If you are doing this exercise in groups, make sure that each child who has experienced loss is in a small group of supportive peers, with a teacher or teaching assistant nearby. Talk to the children about feelings of fear and how hard it is to feel them if they are alone. Tell them that, similar to worries, it is helpful to give fears the light of day so we can chase them away.

2 The second activity, Shrinking My Fears, allows children to try and reduce the big feelings associated with fear, using colour and imagination. Children feel their feelings in their bodies, therefore this exercise makes the connection directly and allows a child to try and find ways to reduce the feelings of fear.

3 Ensure there is enough time given to both exercises, with no need to rush to a new activity at the end.

4 Some children may need time in a quiet space after these exercises, with a safe adult.

Page 2 of 2

Activity 23

Lighting Up Fears Worksheet

👏 Think about one or two fears you have felt that are connected to your loss.

👏 Draw or write these fears in the two light bulbs.

👏 Then colour all around them as light as possible, with yellows and oranges, so that the fears become less strong, less fearful and more bright – fears do not like light!

👏 Tell a teacher or your parent if your fears are too big to feel better after this.

Page 1 of 2

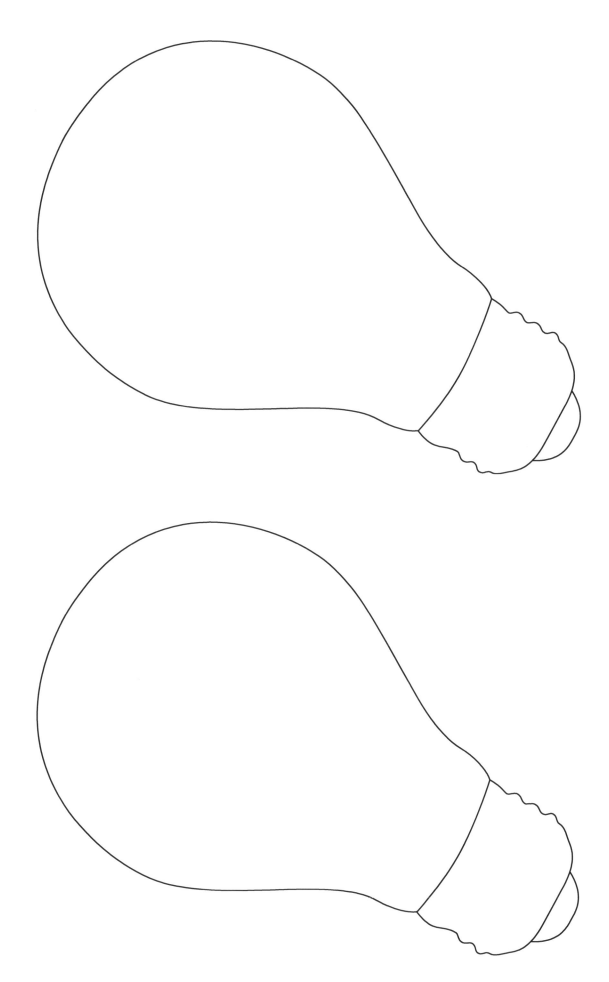

Page 2 of 2

Activity 24
Shrinking My Fears Worksheet

1   Take a minute or two to think of things that make you afraid. Do not take too long on it, because this is not about making yourself afraid but about helping you with the feeling of being afraid.

2   When you have thought of one or more things, see if you can find where you feel that fear in your body – it may be in your tummy, your hands or your feet, for example. Wherever it is, take a deep breath and send the fear to that part of your body.

3   Now, close your eyes and feel that part of your body and see if you can feel the fear as a shape and a colour. Get it as solid as you can.

4   When you are ready, and you know what shape and colour it is, draw the shape and the colour of the fear in the first square.

5   Next close your eyes again and return to feeling the place in your body where you felt the fear. If you need to, take another deep breath and send the fear to that part of your body again.

6   This time imagine a colour and a shape that helps to make the fear smaller and shrinks the first colour and shape.

7   Allow this new colour and shape to become stronger and stronger, so that the first colour and shape are shrunk – or even completely disappear.

8   Then draw this new shape and colour in the second box.

Page 1 of 3

9 Now, if you can, think back to the fear you first thought of, and check if it still feels so fearful. If it does, think of the new second colour and shape and fill your body with this colour until it helps the feeling of fear and makes it go away.

10 Use this exercise for each fear you have.

11 If you still have your fear, tell your teacher or another trusted adult about it.

2 – The Shape and Colour to Shrink and Destroy Fear

1 – The Shape and Colour of Fear

Stories & Memories

Activities 25-28

Telling My Story & Treasuring My Memories

Guidance notes

 To enhance a child's ability to make sense of their loss by storytelling and keeping their memories safe.

Materials

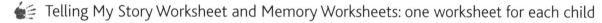 Telling My Story Worksheet and Memory Worksheets: one worksheet for each child

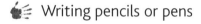 Writing pencils or pens

---

Children who have been bereaved need to tell their own story of their loss. This helps them make sense of it as they move through various stages of development, as well as ensuring that they do not forget the person they have lost. Their need to tell the story, whether it is to their family, another person or just to themselves, has been shown to make a difference to their ability to adjust to the loss.

In a similar way, those children who have experienced significant loss from other causes, such as moving into the care system or a difficult divorce, benefit from telling their story. Those in the care system are often encouraged to do 'life-story work', which is another way to phrase this need to tell their own story. It is crucially important because it helps these children to place themselves in the context of their family history, loss and culture, as well as to adjust to the new environment.

In order for them to tell the story, children may sometimes need to refer back to their relatives for details they may not know, or to objects in their possession whose significance they may not fully understand. Making a memory box, memory journal, memory jar, or any another means of consolidating memories, is a vital way to help children adjust to their loss. The activities that

Page 1 of 2

follow aim to enhance a child's telling of their own story and to enable them to treasure their memories, in order that they can understand their losses and use their experiences as reference points along their life's journey.

The first activity can also be used for children who have not experienced a loss, in order for them to imagine what it may feel like. You can use the scenarios given earlier in Activity 3: Feelings Faces & Scenarios, or make up your own: the children themselves may have their own ideas for stories. This is a creative activity with a purpose: to help a child to either make sense of their own loss or to empathise with those who have suffered loss.

Remember to prepare the children well and to sit children who have had recent losses with those who are regarded as less vulnerable. Encourage storytelling exercises by reminding the children that all families have at least one story they can be proud of, just in case a child is deep within their own loss and struggling to make sense of their experience.

Page 2 of 2

Activity 25
Telling My Story Worksheet

In order to make sense of your loss, sometimes it is helpful to tell your experience as if it is a story. In this way, you can begin to understand and to remember what you and your family have experienced. Each person's experience of loss is different.

1 There are three parts to this storytelling: 1) The Beginning; 2) The Middle; and 3) Now.

2 On the next page there are three sentences under each number: three possible ways to begin your story, three possible ways to tell the middle of your story, and three possible ways to say what is happening now.

3 Choose one sentence from each number.

4 Then, using your choice of the 'beginning', 'middle' and 'now' sentences, start to tell your own special story on another sheet of paper. It can be as long or as short as you like.

5 If you have not had a particular loss recently, you can make up your own story using the three sentences.

6 When you have finished your story, decide what you would like to do with it: you could share it in the class, keep it in a memory box if you have had a recent loss, include it in a scrapbook of memories, or your teacher could choose a selection to put up on your story wall.

Page 1 of 2

1 Beginning sentences

👆 I don't know what happened at first, but …

👆 I remember something happening, because …

👆 I remember how it all started …

2 Middle sentences

👆 I was able to say goodbye by …

👆 I could not say goodbye because …

👆 I keep thinking I would have liked to say …

3 Now sentences

👆 When I remember that time now I feel …

👆 I like to remember that time because …

👆 I find it hard to remember that time because …

Activity 26

My Important Memories Worksheet

Most people find it important to have some memories of the time spent with the person they have lost. This is true whether this person has died or gone away for some reason. These can help you to feel good about yourself as you grow older.

👋 Think about three important memories that you have of a time when you were with the person you have lost.

👋 If you cannot think of three all at once, just do one or two.

👋 Draw or write down three memories that are good memories of something you did together. You may want to add them to a book or box of memories if you have one.

Memory 1

Memory 2

Memory 3

171

Activity 27

My Important Memories 2 Worksheet

What is your earliest memory? Draw or write it here.

What is your very best memory ever of something happening in your family?
Draw or write it here.

Your memories are very important to you. No one can take them away and writing
or drawing them keeps them alive inside you.

Activity 28
Stories of Loss

Guidance notes

In this final storytelling exercise you will find the beginning of a number of small stories that children can use to consider how they would react to the situations in the stories. They can be used for general lessons on loss and bereavement and for circle-time development of empathy. They are suitable for a number of different situations.

- They can be used if a child is recently bereaved and a teacher would like to encourage the class to understand what they are experiencing. Use them for teaching, as opposed to support for those experiencing loss and bereavement.

- They can be used to teach about loss and the feelings associated with loss, by talking about the responses at the end of each paragraph.

- They can be used to discuss what children may need to know when loss happens, to enable empathy and resilience.

- They can be used to help the children create their own stories, by imagining what it would be like if they were the children in the stories. This is an excellent way of enabling empathy and insights into the feelings and needs associated with loss.

- Finally, they can be used to find out if specific children who have experienced loss need more support. A child's reactions and answers to the questions about what is needed and how the characters in the stories feel can reveal their own needs.

Stories of Loss Worksheet

1 Imagine you have a loved pet hamster and it has just died. You tell your mum you want to have it buried, because you used to have lots of cuddles with him. But your mum does not understand and tells you not to be silly, it was only a hamster. What do you do? How will you feel? What do you need?

2 Your grandma, who you do not see very often, rings up to tell your mum that she is very ill and does not have long to live. Your mum comes off the phone crying, but you don't really know your grandma as you only see her once a year. What do you say to Mum? What do you do? What do you need?

3 Your mum and dad are having a few arguments and you are very worried that they may separate, as other friends have told you that sometimes when parents argue it means this could happen. You tell your mum you are worried one night, and she tells you that she and your dad are fine, it's just normal arguments. Do you believe her? How do you feel? What do you need?

4 You get home from school to see a lot of police cars and ambulances around. You knock on your door and a neighbour answers it. You run in and are relieved to see your mum and sister there. However, they then tell you that a neighbour has been run over and it was awful. You knew this neighbour quite well, as she used to look after you. What do you feel? What do you say? What do you need?

5 You have a friend who tells you his dad has had to go to prison, though he does not know why. Your friend seems to think the family will see him again soon, but you have overheard the adults saying he may be away for a year or more. What do you do? What do you say?

6 One evening over your evening meal, your mum and dad tell you that your mum has taken on a new job, and this means you will all have to move home and town. How do you feel? What do you say? What do you need?

Asking Questions
Activities 29–30

Guidance notes

This section allows children to ask the questions they need to ask; all children need to ask questions at some point during an experience of loss.

- These exercises are most suitable for use with individual children who have experienced a loss of some sort.

- Introduce the first exercise by saying that sometimes children have questions they find it hard to ask their family, because they may not want to upset someone. Now is their time to think of any questions they have in relation to a loss they have experienced.

- The second exercise offers suggested questions related to death and dying, which all children may have. They can look at the list and decide if they would like to have answers to any of these questions. It may be that they feel they need answers to all of the questions.

- Remember that some of the children may be able to answer some of the questions themselves, so give them an opportunity to do so if they wish.

Activity 29
Questions About Loss Worksheet

👆 You may have questions about what has happened to you.

👆 Sometimes it is hard to find someone to ask, or you are worried about upsetting someone.

👆 Write down three questions about your loss that you have not been able to ask yet.

1 _____

_____

_____

2 _____

_____

_____

3 _____

_____

_____

Is there someone you would like to answer these questions? _____

Try asking your teacher to help you find the answers.

Activity 30

Questions on Death & Dying Worksheet

👆 Sometimes it is hard to find someone to answer questions about death.

👆 You may have questions about the death of someone you loved.

👆 You may have questions if you know someone else who has experienced the death of someone close.

👆 Make a cross next to any of the questions you would like to know the answer to.

👆 Then add your own answer if you have an idea, on the line below. If you haven't got an answer you don't need to write anything.

1 What happens when someone dies?

_____

2 Did the person know they were dying?

_____

3 Was the person in pain when they died?

_____

4 What is cremation?

_____

Page 1 of 2

5 What is a funeral?

_____

6 What happens to the body when someone dies?

_____

7 Can someone come back when they have died?

_____

8 How do we know when someone has died?

_____

9 Where does someone go when they die?

_____

10 Have you got any other questions to do with death?

_____

Your teacher will help you to find the answers to these questions.

Chapter 7
Resources

A Sample School Bereavement Policy

- Establish contact with the family (either by phone, letter or home visit) when a child experiences bereavement or loss due to any significant cause.

- Establish who in the school the family wishes to be informed about the bereavement: this is sometimes just the head or class teacher, but it could be the entire staff, the child's friends, their entire class or even the whole school.

- Find out what the child has been told as soon as possible, so that others can support them and avoid telling them something they do not already know. This is particularly important for losses such as suicide, because families often do not tell children the details immediately.

- Offer support from a key person in the school. This can be a person who already has responsibility as a key bereavement supporter, or someone specific to this child and family. This person should not be someone who has had a recent bereavement themselves.

- Give guidance as to whether a child should return to school, have work sent home to them, or put aside all school work for the time being. This will depend on the child's reaction to the loss, the family's wishes and the temperament of the child. Many children like to remain as normal as possible immediately after a loss and to see their friends. Others find it impossible to be normal as they are too upset, although they may dip into and out of their feelings.

- Offer a time-out card (see template, p.183) once a child returns to school; this gives the child permission to leave a classroom or another school activity, should they feel the need, without asking permission on each occasion.

- Give a child choices in the first few weeks: specifically who to go to (if not the person already allocated) if they need to leave class when they are upset, lose concentration, or have some other problem.

- Ensure there is support for the child if they wish this; do this discreetly, for example, checking if they want close friends nearby, want to be quiet at playtime, and so on.

- Support the child at the time of the funeral, offering to send a teacher to the funeral if the family would like that. Many families appreciate this gesture, especially if the school is an important base in the community.

- Do not avoid talking about death and loss; allow this as a possible conversation with the bereaved child and others if needed.

Page 1 of 2

- Remember that the pain from loss does not simply stop after a few months. Create a list of anniversaries the child will have to face: birthdays, date of death, Christmas, Mother's and Father's Day. The list can become a file that will follow the child through their life at the school. Monitor, in particular, when the child changes classes, and keep new teachers informed of the child's circumstances.

- Monitor if the child shows particular distress over a period of time and offer extra support if needed.

- Keep in touch with the family over the first few months in particular. Check if significant changes occur in the family life as a result of the loss. If the bereavement was a particularly shocking or sudden loss, issues of grief may not occur for a few months.

- Monitor the impact of more than one bereavement in a class/school community. If necessary, offer a whole school assembly on bereavement and loss.

- Keep a list of local and national resources for guidance, extra support and information if needed.

Page 2 of 2

Template for a Letter to a Family Following Bereavement

Dear _____

We were very sorry to hear of your recent loss. We are writing to express our support as a community to you and your family, and to ask if there is anything we can offer in the way of particular support at this time.

When a child in our care experiences a bereavement, we usually like to support you in a way that suits your circumstances. If you could, do let us know how we can do this, including what [name of child] understands has happened, so that we can support him/her at this most difficult time. We will take our guidance from you as to how to tell the class, his/her friends and the school community.

We can choose a key person within the school for [name of child] to go to whenever he/she needs extra support while in school, as well as a 'time-out' card that he/she can use whenever he/she feels they need to leave lessons. We try and tell all staff who know [name of child], so that they can support him/her as needed.

Please feel you can ring us at any point if you would like to talk through any particular needs you believe [name of child] may have at this time. He/she may be very upset, or tired, and may also need a few days off school. Please be assured that this is normal. [Name of child] may, however, also wish to return to school and see his/her friends, to be reminded of other things and forget his/her loss. We will support whatever decisions you may make regarding attendance at school at this time, and will offer extra support in school if [name of child's] wish is to return immediately.

With our sincerest condolences,

[Name of head teacher/person signing on behalf of the school]

Template for a Time-Out Card

Time-Out Card for _____

This card is to give permission for _____ to leave class whenever he/she needs to without permission.

They will go to _____ [give specific name of room/reception] or meet _____ [name of member of staff].

If _____ is very upset, he/she is allowed to take a close friend with them.

_____ has promised to use this card only when needed, but there is no limit to the number of times it can be used.

It will be reviewed weekly.

_____

[Signature of head teacher/class teacher]

Plan for a General Assembly Focusing on Bereavement

- Begin with a brief talk about death and dying. A suggested opening line might be: 'We hope that someone close to us never dies, but sometimes this happens. We are going to think about this and talk about what happens, and how families say goodbye.'

- For younger children, remind the children that everyone has to die sometimes, and most people die when they are very old. Mention that pets die, animals die in the wild, and aspects of nature die, such as leaves and plants. In spring new shoots are found which give new hope, though the old leaves never return to life. This reassures children that this is a normal cycle of life, and not one to be afraid of. If it is possible, have a table somewhere in the school with different aspects of nature laid out on it, so that children can touch dead leaves, pieces of wood, a live plant, and so on.

- Continue by describing the rituals surrounding death in different religions and parts of the world, such as the Mexican Day of the Dead. Do not forget to mention what happens in the UK.

- If you wish, refer to Christian beliefs and customs, but remember that there are now many beliefs and customs in the UK.

- Remind the children that children and families all over the world mourn and grieve for their loved ones. We are all the same.

- Mention some feelings that children and families can have when they lose someone they love: sadness, anger, fear, upset, worry.

- Finish with a minute's silence or a piece of music to show respect for anyone in the school who has lost a loved one.

- If the family have given permission, you can use the name of the family or child who has lost someone.

- If not, do not mention names and use this time as a group experience to remember all children around the world who have lost someone important.

- As the children leave the hall, try to arrange that a good piece of music is played to wordlessly acknowledge the feelings and impressions connected to death.

Suggestions for Further Reading

Brown L.K. & Brown M., 1998, *When Dinosaurs Die*, Little, Brown Books for Young Readers, London.

> This is a very accessible, readable book with cartoon characters of dinosaurs that talk, ask questions related to death and show emotions such as anger and sadness; they even have mini-funerals for pets!

Burningham J., 2003, *Granpa*, Red Fox, Random House London.

> A picture story of how a child makes sense of his grandpa dying. It is a visual book with few words, to help convey the atmosphere of the loss.

Crossley D., 2000, *Muddles, Puddles and Sunshine*, Winston's Wish, Cheltenham.

> This book is A4, colourful, creative, and full of artistic ideas connected to how a child experiences grief.

Ganerie A. 2006, *Buddhism (This is my Faith)*, Tick Tock Media Ltd, Kent.

> This is an introductory book on Buddhism for older children, exploring the key concepts in a child-friendly way.

Goldman J., 2008, *Uncle Monarch and the Day of the Dead*, Boyds Mill Press, Pennsylvania.

> A lovely tale of a child who is facing the loss of her uncle and using the Day of the Dead celebrations from Mexico to adjust, picture book format.

Halliday N., 2006, *The Lonely Tree*, Halliday Books, Aylesbury.

> A beautifully illustrated picture book following the cycles of nature and trees to explore themes of loss and regeneration.

Heegaard M., 1988, *When Someone Very Special Dies*, Woodland Press, New York.

> A very well-established workbook that allows a child to draw their own experience of loss.

Heegaard M., 1988, *When Something Terrible Happens*, Woodland Press, New York.

> A workbook for non-specific but traumatic loss, similar to the above workbook.

Ironside V., 2004, *The Huge Bag of Worries*, Hodder Children's Books, London.

> A hugely successful book to be used with all children experiencing worries, for whatever cause, but typically due to issues such as loss and bereavement. It is a story, but it encourages a child to share their worries so that they can be sorted into those that need attention and those that will disappear on their own.

Jacobs A., 2013a, *Changes: a story to help young children with change and loss*, Hinton House, Buckingham.

> A moving book introducing the concepts of loss and change to very young children, through simple, clear language and beautiful illustrations.

Jacobs A., 2013b, *Lucy's Story: a child's story of grief and loss*, Hinton House, Buckingham.

> An illustrated, therapeutic story written from the point of view of a young girl whose father has died.

Miles L. & Jacobs A., 2013, *Supporting Fostered and Adopted Children through Grief and Loss*, Hinton House, Buckingham.

> A wealth of ideas and creative approaches for use with children from the care system who have often experienced multiple losses.

Rosen M., 2011, *Michael Rosen's Sad Book*, Walker Books, London.

> A book (fantastically illustrated by Quentin Blake) that reflects the sadness we all feel when we experience loss, written in memory of Michael Rosen's son.

Simmons P., 1998, *Fred*, Red Fox, London.

> A wonderful, light-hearted book about a cat who dies and whose neighbourhood cat friends come to the garden to remember his life.

Stickney D., *Waterbugs and Dragonflies*, Pilgrim Press, Cleveland, Ohio.

> A small paperback book to help children understand the natural process of death and dying.

Sunderland M., 2003, *The Day the Sea Went out and Never Came Back*, Speechmark Publishing, Milton Keynes.

> An illustrated tale to help children make sense of loss by using the images of sea and the sand dragon who mourns the sea when it fails to come back in again.

Thomas S., 2000, *I Miss You*, Wayland Publishing, London.

> A well-illustrated book for very young children who are trying to come to terms with the loss of a close relative.

Varley S., 1992, *Badger's Parting Gift*, HarperCollins, New York.

> A picture book introducing the story of badger and what happens in his community after his death in a very non-threatening way.

Helpful Websites

www.winstonswish.org.uk

> Winston's Wish, the Gloucester-based charity, has an interactive website for children to use, as well as resources such as books and memory boxes for sale. It has a helpline, an online resource to support school professionals and a comprehensive list of books for bereaved children.

www.childbereavement.org.uk

> Child Bereavement is one of the main UK bereavement organisations supporting bereaved children and parents. It offers training courses, individual support, group support and some resources.

www.childhoodbereavementnetwork.org.uk

> The foremost charity supporting bereaved children in the UK. It is involved in policy-making, holds a list of all bereavement services for children in the UK, and offers resources for children (such as cards to be given to a child when they are bereaved).

www.crusebereavementcare.org.uk

> National charity supporting bereaved adults and children; it provides details of services for children and offers children's bereavement support in some areas of the UK. All their workers are volunteers trained with Cruse.

www.dyingmatters.org

> A government-led initiative that offers some excellent resources for children and families to approach conversations about death and dying.

www.netmums.com

> Their website has an excellent page on bereavement, aimed at parents supporting their children.

References

Astley N., 2003, *Do Not Go Gentle*, Bloodaxe Books, Northumberland.

Atkinson M., 2009, *Healing Touch for Children: Massage, Reflexology and Acupressure for children from 4–12 years old*, Gaia/Octopus Publishing, London.

Bowlby J., 1969, *Attachment and Loss*, Vol. 1, Hogarth Press, London.

Dyregrov A., 1991, *Grief in Children: A Handbook for Adults*, Jessica Kingsley, London.

Gibran K., 1923, *The Prophet*, Wm Heinemann, London.

Harrison L. & Harrington R., 2001, 'Adolescents' Bereavement Experiences: Prevalence, Association with Depressive Symptoms, and Use of Services', *Journal of Adolescence* 24, pp159–69.

Klass et al. (eds), 1996, *Continuing Bonds*, Taylor & Francis, Washington, DC.

Kübler-Ross E., 1969, *On Death and Dying*, Touchstone, New York.

Milne A.A., 1929, *Winnie-the-Pooh*, Methuen Children's Books, London.

Oliver, M., 1983, 'In Blackwater Woods', in *American Primitive*, Little, Brown & Co., Boston, MA.

Perry B.D. & Hambrick E., 2008, 'The Neurosequential Model of Therapeutics', *Reclaiming Children and Youth* 17.3, pp38–43.

Roffey S., 2006, *Circle Time for Emotional Literacy*, Sage, London.

Roger J.E. (ed.), 2007, *The Art of Grief*, Routledge, Taylor & Francis, New York.

Schuurman D., 2003, *Never the Same*, St Martin's Press, New York.

Shipman et al., 2001, 'Responding to the Needs of Schools in Supporting Bereaved Children', *Bereavement Care* 20 (3), pp6–7.

Silverman P.R. & Worden J.W., 1992, 'Children's Reactions in the Early Months After the Death of a Parent', *American Journal of Orthopsychiatry* 162 (1), pp93–104.

Stokes J., 2004, *Then, Now and Always*, Winston's Wish, Cheltenham.

Stroebe M.S. & Schut H.?., 1999, 'The Dual Process Model of Coping with Bereavement: Rationale and Description', *Death Studies* 23, p.197.

Sunderland M., 2008, *What Every Parent Needs to Know*, Dorling Kindersley, London.

Willis J., 1992, *Toffee Pockets*, Bodley Head/Red Fox, Random House Group Ltd, London.

Worden W.J., 1996, *Children and Grief*, The Guildford Press, New York.

Also available from Hinton House

Supporting Fostered & Adopted Children through Grief & Loss
Practical Ideas & Creative Approaches

NEW! for 2013 · **All ages**

Lorna Miles & Anna Jacobs

Creative ideas and guidance for carers, social care staff and school professionals.

A child from the care system experiences multiple losses: family, home, friends, familiar environments and sometimes also bereavement. They can be confused about what is happening and what the future holds.

This book covers theory, understanding of the developmental and traumatic influences which have shaped children's behaviour and will provide hope to carers and others who offer this vital care.

Containing a wealth of ideas and creative approaches to encourage conversation and interaction, this resource aims to help children and those supporting them with emotions, relationships and behaviours using a range of mediums such as art, creative writing, storytelling and film.

192pp A4 paperback • 978-1906531-62-1 • **£29.99**

Supporting Teenagers through Grief & Loss

NEW! for 2013 · **Ages 11-16+**

Anna Jacobs

Understand how adolescents experience loss and how to provide help and support.

Helpful advice, worksheets and suggestions to support young people in their experience of loss in its many forms. Teenagers perceive and experience loss differently from younger children and need support and understanding at home and in school.

- Explores how adolescents understand & respond to loss.
- Explains the needs of teenagers facing loss at different stages of grief.
- Provides guidance on monitoring if extra support is needed.
- Contains a toolkit of creative age-appropriate resources exploring feelings, behaviours, thoughts & memories.
- Gives clear guidance on what to say and how to respond.
- Is suitable for use in groups or with individuals.
- Can be used alongside the therapeutic book Rory's Story.

Invaluable for teachers and school assistants and can also be used by social services and health professionals, parents and carers.

192pp A4 paperback • 978-1906531-59-1 • **£24.99**

Lucy's Story
A child's story grief and loss

Ages 6-11 · **NEW! for 2013**

Anna Jacobs

Once there was a happy child who had no cares and worries. She had a lovely mum, a wonderful dad, and a baby brother. But then it all went horribly wrong...

This illustrated therapeutic story is written from the point of view of a young girl whose father has died. It explores how she feels and reacts to the loss both within her family and at school, and shows how an isolated child such as Lucy can be given help and understanding.

Offers an explanation of the concepts of death and loss, and shows how children experience loss.

Can be used by schools, counsellors and families to support children who are experiencing loss, as well as to safely introduce concepts of bereavement within the classroom. Each chapter contains notes related to the issues of bereavement and loss with children of primary age.

36pp illustrated paperback • 978-1906531-60-7 • **£12.99**

Rory's Story
An Adolescent Story of Grief and Loss

NEW! for 2013 · **Ages 13+**

Anna Jacobs

'Rory picked himself up and looked down: his hands were full of gravel and blood... things were different now and he didn't know what to do about it...'

Rory is an adolescent boy who is struggling with the loss of his mother. Confused and bullied at school, he attempts to run away and finally returns to face his feelings.

This therapeutic story:

- Is a gritty, readable story that teenagers will relate to.
- Explores the teenage experience of loss and bereavement.
- Can be used to support young people who have experienced loss.
- Will help teenagers understand the needs of their peers when loss occurs.
- Has notes for discussion on the themes of each chapter.

This useful tool which will help teachers, therapists and carers to support and understand the needs of adolescents facing loss.

48pp A5 paperback • 978-1906531-42-3 • **£12.99**

Changes
A story to help young children when loss or change occurs

Anna Jacobs

Ages 3-7 · **NEW! for 2013**

This moving, simple book introduces the concepts of loss and change to very young children. It uses the power of nature to explain what loss may feel like, and uses simple, clear language which will aid understanding and discussion of feelings.

It is beautifully illustrated throughout and aims to build resilience in very young children by offering them hope, as well as suggesting ways to help difficult feelings. Because it is non-specific, it can be used with many different forms of loss, such as divorce and separation, bereavement and even moving house.

24pp Illustrated paperback • 978-1906531-41-6 • **£9.99**

www.hintonpublishers.com   e: **sales@hintonpublishers.com**   HINTONHOUSE

t: **+44 (0)1280 822557**   f: **+44 (0)560 3135274**